WHEN CATHOLICS MARRY AGAIN

A Guide for the Divorced, Their Families, and Those Who Minister to Them

Gerald S. Twomey

WINSTON PRESS

Library of Congress Catalog Card Number: 82-70487

ISBN: 0-86683-633-0

Printed in the United States of America.

5 4 3 2 1

Winston Press, Inc.
430 Oak Grove
Minneapolis, Minnesota 55403

Special thanks to Professor John Swanstrom for permission to use his untitled painting (the original is six feet square) in the front cover design. Swanstrom is on the faculty of Central Michigan University in Mount Pleasant, Michigan.

CONTENTS

PART FOUR   ADJUSTING TO A NEW LIFE-STYLE

FOREWORD

Count as lost those tears
that turn no mill.

—Edna St. Vincent Millay

The poets capture for us the meaning of life in all its aspects, and them frame it in words that sometimes haunt and prod. It seems to me that there is no greater loss than lost tears, unredeemed pain; no greater tragedy in human life than the repetition of mistakes. To have set out again and come back to the same place and never know how one arrived there either time is a sign that God is inviting us to prayer and self-reflection. It is important that we individually and collectively need never shed tears that "turn no mill."

Because we live in an age when the family has been called the "number one disaster area," partly because divorce has increased more rapidly than any other societal phenomenon, the false assumption might be made that we have been equally skilled in acquiring and developing the insights we need to facilitate the divorce adjustment process. Quite the contrary is true. Just as the individual divorcing person is often overwhelmed with all that is happening both practically and emotionally, so those seeking to help with the divorce adjustment process continue to receive new data at a rate that makes it difficult to reflect helpful information back in a usable fashion.

Having just completed ten years working with divorcing people throughout the North American continent, I continue to learn and to realize that every divorce is different as is every marriage. No two people experience divorce in the same manner;

and the steps to new life, while similar in some ways, retain qualities unique to each person.

I believe that divorce is one of the greatest evils of our time; yet for some it is the only way to avoid further destruction of persons. Divorce does not solve problems; it simply exchanges one set of challenges for another. The output of energy in recovering after divorce is not less than the energy expended in struggling with a marriage that is faltering; it may indeed be greater. Yet, for some persons, divorce is the only human way to redirect the pain into life-giving channels.

Because marriage and family life are such all-encompassing realities, the end of a marriage places the divorcing person in the position of needing to deal with nearly every significant aspect of life. It means dealing with some of life's most important questions at a time when one's physical and emotional levels may be at an all-time low. It is for this reason that divorcing people need every resource available. It is also for this reason that people in professions that can help people objectify their experience continue to read and reflect and write in order to help divorcing people find meaning in their tragic and traumatic time of loss.

DIVORCE AS A PROCESS

A key understanding about divorce is the realization that it is not an event. Divorce is a process that begins long before two people separate or see a lawyer, and it continues long after the judge has made the final pronouncement. Unless the divorcing person understands this, there is danger of undue personal concern that shows itself in a fearsome statement that I have heard from hundreds: "I've not only lost my marriage; now I'm losing my mind." Unless those helping with the divorce adjustment process understand that it involves grieving and requires time, the difficult but important challenges may not be offered.

The divorce process may begin when two people begin to avoid conflict or fail to share their feelings. It may begin because one or both parties do not make the necessary investment in a self-discovery process which is at the heart of growing in friendship. The divorce process may even begin at the time of the marriage because sometimes people enter into marriage with inadequate self-images and with hidden expectations which not only prevent growing together but may even destroy the possibility of friendship.

But whenever the divorce process begins, it is not likely that any person will grow through it and come to new life without information and the caring and supportive presence of others. It is the nature of Christianity that we are called to live in relationship, we are called to share. For us, as Christians, the realization that we neither grow nor heal in isolation may come to us most clearly in times of suffering when we are left powerless and must draw our strength from others.

Divorce touches every life. None of us can escape this tragedy as it touches the life of a relative, friend, co-worker, neighbor, or casual acquaintance. For many it has always seemed like something that happened to someone else. For many, divorce has been a place of judgment. Like a young man at a recent retreat for divorcing people who asked to apologize to the group at the end of the closing Eucharist. He said, "Last year when I saw that this retreat house was offering a weekend retreat for separated and divorced Catholics, I said to my wife, 'What's wrong with those folks? Anyone can make a marriage work if they just work hard enough at it.' And now," he said, "I stand before you as a newly separated and badly hurting man. I'm so sorry that I judged you, and I'm afraid of the judgments of others."

It is an oft-told story, a story that can have a happy ending only if all of us take seriously our personal responsibilities to love and care for one another. We need not fear that we are "condoning" divorce, for divorce remains what it is: an evil in our society, an evil we wish everyone might avoid. Rather we must look upon ourselves as a people called to be present to others at a singularly tragic moment and to walk with them through the many long miles of the divorce adjustment process.

It is important that no Christian simply *go through* the divorce process. The message of the death and resurrection of Jesus calls each person to *grow through* divorce.

If one simply *goes* through a divorce, there is great likelihood that one may be caught in some place of non-life along the way—may be caught in the denial, anger, bitterness, depression, or blaming that are a part of grieving. Unless one has good information and the presence of supportive friends one may repeat past patterns in a second relationship that will make a second marriage a place of pain not unlike the first.

Because we have not understood the process of divorce, neither the Church, the helping professions, nor society in general has been helpful to divorcing people and their families. It is a part of the mystery of God's love that the Catholic Church, which was more vocal than any other in condemning not only the evil of divorce and, unfortunately, even divorcing people, has given leadership to other churches and even to the secular counseling world in discovering the keys to new life and the importance of a support system for divorcing people.

From the year 1972, when I began my work with divorcing Catholics, until the present time I have seen the state of the question transformed in the Catholic Church from "Why should we give pastoral care to divorcing people?" to "How can we best support and care for divorcing people?"

GROWING THROUGH THE DIVORCE PROCESS TO A PLACE OF NEW LIFE

In the past ten years I have discovered that there is only one human tragedy greater than a divorce, and that is a second divorce. The people who have walked this way tell me repeatedly and without exception that the second divorce was much more destructive for them and much more painful.

This fact coupled with a statistic published in a newsletter titled *Marriage and Divorce Today* is of great concern—the concern at the heart of this book. The statistics read: "80% of divorcing people choose to remarry, 50% of them within the first twelve months after their divorce." I have met thousands of divorcing people throughout the United States and Canada, people of all faiths and cultural backgrounds. Nothing is more certain for me than the fact that no person is ready for remarriage twelve months after a divorce. Marriage is not like a coat that we put on and remove with ease. Rather, it is like a tapestry two people weave together. It is a tapestry woven in such a way that two people committed to their relationship can no longer identify which threads were given by whom. In a divorce this tapestry is torn apart; the reclaiming of a personal identity simply cannot be achieved in a short time. It is all too human but potentially destructive for a person to choose remarriage as a solution to the personal pain that inevitably follows in the wake of divorce.

Just as marriage is a basic human right, so, too, is remarriage. It is sometimes impossible for a newly separated or divorced person to understand why the first question to be dealt with is not "Can I remarry?" but rather "How do I know where I am along that growth process after divorce so that I will have some signs of when I am ready to remarry?"

The key to the healing process lies in discovering where a person is with himself or herself. The strongest assurance for readiness for a marriage, whether a first or a second marriage, is a healthy self identity. One of the surest signs that a divorcing person has grown along the journey through divorce is the difference between the initial statements that reflect a near compulsion to remarry and the healed stance that says, "I like myself better than I ever have. I'm open to remarrying some day if that's possible, but if it never happens I know I'll be just fine."

At the heart of every divorce is the same question that is indicative of readiness to marry again. It is a key to the importance of Gerry Twomey's work when he says, "The key to authentic relationships is the ability to rebuild one's level of competency and self-esteem and to foster mutually satisfying relationships."

He says further, "To recover from a crisis of loss, one has to be willing to invest in oneself and others. One has to be willing to learn to love again." I would add that when a divorcing person has walked that journey, long and self-demanding though it may be, that person may have learned many of love's most important lessons for the first time.

Gerry Twomey's book is a monumental contribution to the journey through divorce to the possibility of considering a second marriage. Its nearly all-encompassing scope gathers into one place not only the most important questions but also the experience and insight related to them. It seems incomprehensible that a person would have been faithful to the journey through this work and not have touched on the most important issues and potential pitfalls to a second and happy marriage.

Gerry Twomey's work is added insurance that, in each individual divorcing person's life, the tears are sacred and the pain redemptive.

Paula Ripple, F.S.P.A.
President
Franciscan Sisters of Perpetual Adoration

PREFACE

A little more than a year ago I was surprised to find a letter in my mailbox from Cyril A. Reilly, Trade Editor at Winston Press. It began: "Your recent review of Walter Kasper's *Theology of Christian Marriage* mentioned the many basic questions not covered in his book. Here at Winston Press we are always looking for books that do treat such fundamental topics as Christian marriage. We were wondering if you would be interested in doing such a book (or books?) for us. . . ."

My initial reaction was a mixture of surprise, flattery, and apprehension. Since my overriding belief is that books of theology should stem from one's own experience and that contemporary theologies of Christian marriage might therefore best flow from those who are themselves married, I begged off the request. But a gnawing feeling stemming from my experience in active ministry kept telling me that "the many basic questions not covered" in Catholic marriage guides concerning the needs of divorced persons needed to be dealt with. I hope this book will begin to serve that need for many.

The consistent interest, support, and encouragement lent to the project by my editor, Cy Reilly, ensured its completion and sharpened its focus immeasurably. The book came at his invitation and in some ways is as much his work as my own.

I owe a special debt to Sister Paula Ripple and Father James Young, who more than anyone else have advanced the pastoral issues discussed in this book. Support groups for separated, divorced, or widowed Catholics at Holy Trinity Church in Georgetown, St. Anthony Church in Oceanside, Long Island, and St. John Nepomucene Church in Bohemia, Long Island, helped to refine my views and sensitize me to the personal and pastoral needs and dreams of persons preparing for remarriage.

The encouragement and support of many persons affirmed me in pursuing and completing this work, and I particularly appreciate the interest shown by my family, the people and parish staff of St. John Nepomucene Church, and my old friends and mentors, Bill Cook and Ron Herzman. I am particularly grateful to my bishop, Most Reverend John McGann, for the support he has shown me in this and all pastoral undertakings.

The staffs of the St. Joseph's College and Connetquot Public Libraries provided a quiet place for research and writing. My cousin, Clare Kelly, generously typed portions of the manuscript. To all these persons, and others too numerous to mention here, I am deeply grateful.

This book is dedicated, with esteem and affection, to Jim and the late Pat Dunne, who more than anyone else convinced me of the value and need for such a guide.

Gerald S. Twomey

Part One

COMING TO TERMS WITH BEING SINGLE AGAIN

1

THE END OF A MARRIAGE: A CRISIS OF LOSS

The death knell of a marriage sounds with finality. Whether we hear the clattering of gravel and earth atop a coffin lid at a graveside service or watch a signature dry on a rescript of divorce in a judge's chambers, the practical upshot is in large measure the same. Two lives lived together have been put asunder. What once may have been alive and vibrant is now lifeless. A marriage has died.

Sooner or later, all marriages end here on earth. Yet whatever the cause, the end of a marriage is necessarily a trauma in anyone's life. In no other human relationship, association, or institution does a person's intense desire to know and be known, to love and be loved possessively and exclusively find such expression and fulfillment as in marriage. The deep human need for inclusion and intimacy, fulfilled in the mutual trust, interest, and love found in a happy marriage, produces a kind of *bonding* of persons unmatched in other relationships. Paradoxically, even marriages that seemed doomed from the start trigger an awareness of that now-broken bonding when they die. The death of a marriage always signals an intense crisis of loss.

The end of a marriage is a *crisis* of *loss*. It prompts the loss of many things near and dear to a person: identity, friendship, sexual intimacy, a secure place in a family grouping, inclusion in social activities. More often than not, the death of a spouse or the ending of a marriage through separation or divorce also paves the way for a wave of accompanying losses, such as the change of domicile or a radical reversal in financial security. Each of these compounding factors is a major loss in its own right and is felt deeply on both the conscious and the unconscious levels.

Some years ago a psychiatrist named Thomas Holmes developed a stress scale to measure the traumatic effects of crises of loss on people. This "Richter scale" was developed on a hundred-point basis. In descending order, the three most traumatic events experienced were the death of a spouse or other immediate family member (low 90s), the end of a marriage through separation or divorce (mid 80s), and the relocation of a household by change of address (high 70s). Since either one of the first two quite often serves to prompt the third and other related crises of loss, it can easily be seen that combinations of such related factors can exact a staggering psychic toll. Holmes noted that if a person's point total exceeded 300 on the scale in a twelve-month period, in 80 cases out of 100 he or she would surely experience some serious mental and physical aftereffects. The findings further showed that 53% of persons registering between 150 and 300 on the stress scale would develop similar problems. Put plainly, the end of a marriage and its accompanying problems often serve to unleash a storm of powerful emotions, with far-reaching and potentially damaging effects.

Typically, the "survivor" is faced with overloaded emotional circuits that affect him or her deeply. A fear of abandonment may fan the anxiety level to a fever pitch. The person often feels victimized and rejected and tends to withdraw further into himself or herself. An overriding sense of guilt, failure, abandonment, remorse, and insecurity may surface. He or she may waste away, feeling helpless, angry, out of touch with reality and lacking a sense of control, tottering on the brink of despair. Such crises often carry with them distorted images of self as well as of others, and these images are complicated by the fact that others tend to avoid the "survivor" and to treat him or her like a pariah. Paradoxically, this experience prompts some persons to withdraw further and to turn in more deeply upon themselves so that they become more distant, more isolated.

Any major experience of loss triggers a disruption of identity, kicks up a flow of feelings from the past (often unresolved hurtful feelings), and releases heightened levels of emotion. This is all an unavoidable part of the pain of being human, a normal part of the grieving process. These feelings are very real, very painful, very human, and very much to be expected. The fact that 37% of all first marriages entered into in the United States end in divorce and that even the happiest and longest-lasting marriages ultimately end in death means that these feelings are experienced by the vast majority of people. Yet in spite of the high frequency of marital dissolution, each individual breakdown remains a real crisis-causer. In the day-to-day world in which we live, far removed from the idealized portraits of the Waltons or of Norman Rockwell, lie the challenges to explore fully the elements of the crises and to find ways of coping with and growing through the wrenching pain caused by the end of a marriage.

And yet, despite all the pain that comes with the breakup of a marriage, it is useful to recall the insight of the ancient Hebrews that every moment of life is charged with elements both of blessing and of curse. The wise person is the one who seeks to maximize the blessings and to offset the impact of the curses in any given instance. In its root sense, the Greek word for *crisis* means "decision." Each person facing a crisis has the capacity to make a decision, to choose, to move beyond the constraints of the present moment and to move onward toward a more promising, hope-filled horizon. To be sure, any crisis of loss is a painful blow, especially when with its attendant losses it is linked to the end of a marriage. But as the characters in the Chinese ideogram for the word *crisis* show so aptly, any crisis brings with it the twin elements of danger and opportunity, with dangers so real and formidable that only a fool would try to minimize them. Still, if the emotional energy triggered by the end of a marriage is not harnessed and translated into constructive behavior, it can be destructive and almost demonic, and it will almost certainly work into deep-seated, counter-productive patterns of self-destructive behavior such as sarcasm, bitterness, resentment, hostility, hatred, loneliness, apathy, or depression.

While the end of a marriage can imperil or ruin an individual or a family, it can also be an opportunity for growth and for an experience of richer life—but only if those involved are willing to come to terms with the past, recognize self-defeating patterns of behavior, and work to change them. Only then can such an unwelcome experience open a person to further possibilities in relationships that will be lasting and mutually enriching. Only then can a person be truly free to love again, to give himself or herself totally to another.

2

FEELINGS TRIGGERED
BY A BROKEN MARRIAGE

To be able to grow by facing a crisis of loss, we must be willing and able to come to grips with the reality of the former relationship and to recognize and accept its passing. We must also try to recognize and minimize self-defeating patterns of behavior that hinder the recovery process, and be willing to invest time and energy constructively to bring about certain changes within ourselves and the surrounding world. This chapter will examine some ways in which people can recognize and face crises of loss while coming to terms with the relationship that has died. It will focus on pitfalls to avoid—common patterns of self-defeating behavior. The basic insight to be offered here is that the death of a marriage releases a flood of negative emotions and that these, if unchecked, can severely undercut the "survivor's" all-important sense of significance, competence, and lovability. We will consider ways of drawing on our personal (internal) and interpersonal (external) resources in order to deal with those negative feelings.

Initially, it is important to realize that grieving is a necessary, functional human experience. Its task, in the words of Shakespeare, is "to give sorrow words," to allow for the constructive expression of the intense feelings triggered by the loss. *Accepting* the loss is far more important than *understanding* it, though ordinarily the acceptance takes a great deal of time and effort. Much groundbreaking work has been done in this area by the noted Swiss psychiatrist Elisabeth Kübler-Ross, well known for her work with the terminally ill and for her writings on death and dying.

Dr. Kübler-Ross's distinctive contribution is her recognition that there are clear phases, or stages, through which most persons pass in coming to terms with any experience of loss. While this insight is hardly an infallible pronouncement carved in stone, it is nonetheless a useful diagnostic tool. In her most famous work, *On Death and Dying,* Dr. Kübler-Ross spells out five stages of death and dying through which people ordinarily pass if sufficient time and caring are offered as they draw closer to death. She dubs the stages denial, anger, depression, bargaining, and acceptance. The important point to note here is that there is a *process*. Grieving requires time and energy and caring to yield a healthy resolution to the crisis of loss. Most experts agree that it takes anywhere from a year (the bare minimum) to four years to recover from the death of a spouse or from a divorce. Recovery means that one has arrived at the final stage of acceptance and has achieved the sense of "having made it" while no longer being dominated by the past. In a nutshell, recovery takes lots of time and energy and the presence of caring persons.

A number of parallels can be drawn between facing one's own death and coming to terms with the realities of a marriage that has died. The end of a marriage, either through death, divorce, or separation, often unleashes a barrage of traumatic shock waves. The initial, instinctive sense of shock and numbness that overcomes the survivor is often followed by a quick sense of denial: "No, it couldn't happen to me." Then a strong surge of anger may surface, often complicated by feelings of guilt. Frequently, the natural human tendency to attempt to strike a bargain appears, directed toward the mate or toward God, in a fleeting attempt to buy more time or to have a second chance to salvage the relationship. If the anger is not dealt with properly, it can be internalized and cause depression. But gradually, as the new reality is tested out and the old reality finally laid to rest, the survivor can establish his or her own independent existence and come to a level of acceptance that the marriage is over. But this takes much time, energy, and loving help to achieve.

In his excellent book *Creative Divorce* (New York: Signet, 1975), divorce adjustment counselor Mel Krantzler speaks of three critical phases through which each person must pass in moving toward the stage of acceptance. First there must be a recognition that the relationship has ended, and then a period of mourning. Krantzler minces no words when he indicates that the person must then "undertake the slow, painful process of emotional readjustment to the fact of single living." Each of these three steps is worthy of careful consideration, since the person who has not recognized and accepted the reality of the death of the marriage will probably never be able to move beyond being mired in the old relationship. Only in the course of time can the necessary healing take place, as the person seeks to reestablish his or her own sense of competency and self-esteem. Only when that sense has been regained can the "opportunity" side of the crisis be actualized and the sense of recovery achieved. Once beyond that point, the person can again enter into meaningful and intimate personal relationships, and in quality these are likely to equal or exceed those of the former marriage.

Some definite cautions are in order. After a marriage ends, people too often fall prey to the "blame game," looking for a scapegoat on whom to pin their own frustrations while failing to assume their fair share of responsibility and to take charge of where they find themselves in the present moment. It is important that such persons be honest with themselves and seek to discover and resolve whatever inner conflicts may have contributed to the unraveling of their marriage or surfaced afterward. The key to authentic recovery is the ability to rebuild one's level of competency and self-esteem and to foster mutually satisfying relationships. Anything that works against these goals must be firmly resisted.

People can change best in the context of a loving, caring, faithful relationship. So they must reestablish mutuality of interests, trust, and affection if the loss is to help them grow. It's not unlike the well-known story of the Wizard of Oz,

where the eccentric, exiled Wizard from Kansas actually suc-
ceeded in offering the Tin Man, Scarecrow, and Cowardly
Lion only what they already possessed within themselves (their
inherent lovability, intelligence, and courage) so that they could
regain a sense of wholeness and overcome their captivity in a
strange land. They did this through their bond of companionship with one another and with Dorothy ("and Toto, too").
Like the characters of Oz, every human being who is willing
to risk and become vulnerable again in a particular relationship
and within the context of a broader support system that can
be a source of life and love can reestablish personal autonomy
and begin to grow and develop more strongly because of the
loss situation. To recover from a crisis of loss, one has to be
willing to invest in oneself and in others. One has to be willing
to learn to love again.

Though it is necessary to reach out and take some definite
positive steps, certain ways of relating need to be avoided. In
the early phases of mourning there is a natural tendency to be
somewhat distant in one's relationships (which is quite acceptable early on), but this tendency should be closely checked
so that one does not cut oneself off detrimentally. Another
pitfall is wallowing in self-pity. While everyone, humanly
speaking, has a certain right to feel sorry for himself or herself
from time to time, the red-flag word here is *wallowing*. Mel
Krantzler puts it well in *Creative Divorce*: "You are probably
wallowing if, after a year or more . . . you are still clinging
to reasons to feel sorry for yourself, and using them as excuses
to avoid taking necessary risks" (p. 107).

People often seek to retain a stranglehold grip on the old
relationship. This usually means that they will muddle present
reality with past relationships, not knowing which is which.
By not checking out the possible negative aspects of the former
relationship, they run the risk of repeating the same self-defeating ways as they try to relate to new people (a process
sometimes called "transference"). When a person is struggling
and feels lost and rejected, it is important that he or she seek
out new friends to supplement the old, friends who might now

more aptly fit the new patterns of needs as the "survivor" approaches the fact of single life again. At this stage, support systems such as church or other interest groups and organizations like Parents Without Partners or Divorced or Separated Catholics can help one expand friendships and head off potentially self-defeating patterns of behavior.

Following the end of a marriage, people commonly have a poor self-image. Ordinarily, in a loss situation the person's feelings of self-worth nose-dive as he or she experiences a sense of inferiority and a distorted view of the self. A while back I was in the throes of an immobilizing depression. I said to a close friend, "I feel as though I have the reverse Midas touch. Everything I touch turns to stone." To others I may have appeared unflappable and in control, but in my gut I felt I was a total failure. This same point was illustrated in the words of a classmate who told me, "You know the Oscar Wilde novel, *The Picture of Dorian Gray,* when at the end the picture is slashed up with a knife by the main character, who sees himself in it. . . ? Sometimes that's the way I feel about myself, too." Such a revelation was mind-boggling to me, since this friend seemed to me to be "together," "intact," "well-integrated." Yet deep within ourselves we are too often the victims of our poor self-images and give in to acute but highly distorted images of ourselves and others. This obviously fosters more entrenched patterns of self-defeating behavior, since to present ourselves persistently as a dishrag or doormat in effect encourages others to treat us accordingly.

In addition to the tendency toward a diminished self-image (with its accompanying distortions), another pattern that crises of loss often set off is the tendency to dig in one's heels and refuse to change established patterns of relating to others. In this vein, a person may attempt to rationalize the posture by limply mumbling that "The devil you know is better than the devil you don't know"—a weak justification for maintaining a dead-end pattern of relating.

Another consequence of the low self-image is the defensiveness with which persons bristle when threatened with insecurity or anxiety. These three factors (inferiority, refusal to change, defensiveness) stifle the possibility of growth in crisis moments such as the end of a marriage. W.H. Auden noted: "Man needs escape as he needs food and deep sleep." In crisis moments none of us would survive without some ways of escape—ways that help deflect the firestorm of negative feelings and enable us finally to come to terms with the realities of the situation. However, we might enter into a number of compulsions as a means of flight from self or from others in order to avoid dealing with the harsh realities of a situation when we feel as though we are "between a rock and a hard place." These include workaholism, abuse of alcohol or drugs, sexual promiscuity, overeating, becoming fixated before the "boob tube," and any number of other ways of anesthetizing ourselves to pain. We must recognize these cultural addictions for what they are and energetically resist them, since they prevent us from dealing with our personal agenda and really using the experience of loss as an opportunity for growth.

It is also very important to be aware of the physical symptoms generated in the body by unresolved negative feelings churned up after a divorce or the death of a spouse. Medical doctors confidently estimate that as much as 80% of all illness is psychosomatically induced, namely, directly linked to unresolved psychic or emotional tension. The body serves as a barometer and as a lightning rod for diffuse, non-directed feelings, manifested in such symptoms as scalp spasms, migraines and other types of headaches, backaches, gastroenteritis, ulcers, colitis, vomiting, diarrhea, heart palpitations, even heart attacks or cancer.

Recent scientific research has indicated a marked correlation between cancer proneness and certain self-defeating patterns of behavior, specifically: (a) a dominant tendency to carry resentment and to withhold forgiveness; (b) a tendency toward self-pity; (c) a poor self-image; and (d) an underdeveloped ability to foster and maintain meaningful long-term relationships. Illness that is organic is nevertheless frequently triggered and prolonged by a lack of love for self and for others. Anxiety, fear, anger, and guilt can all converge to produce profoundly negative changes within a person's biochemical makeup. The research of noted doctors such as Meyer Friedman on heart disease and of O. Carl Simonton on cancer are particularly enlightening in this regard, though they are supported by dozens of journal articles and studies. Simonton has found that cancer often develops within six months to a year after an emotionally stressful experience such as divorce, retirement, or the death of a spouse. He links this phenomenon to the unresolved anger and guilt that eat away at a person's body until eventually the body reacts to the signals and begins to destroy its own cells. All of this is a sobering prelude to saying that the person who is recovering from the death of a marriage must be willing and able to let go of the past relationship, engage in meaningful friendships and loving relationships, and work to minimize self-defeating behavior while seeking to reestablish his or her own sense of competency and self-esteem. In the next chapter we will focus on the predominant emotions of anxiety, depression, anger, guilt, and loneliness— five common and potentially crippling responses to the end of a marriage.

3

EMOTIONAL ADJUSTMENT: COPING WITH ANXIETY, DEPRESSION, ANGER, GUILT, AND LONELINESS

Anxiety has been called the "disease of the age," and indeed it is rampant in North American society. Anxiety can basically be understood as a signal that the ego sends out to warn of some kind of internal conflict. It is often based on fear and coupled with a sense of loss: of position or social or economic status, of power, prestige, or possessions. Classically, psychology has seen anxiety as falling under two headings: normal (healthy) and neurotic (excessive). Moderate anxiety is both normal and useful, and it helps a person come to terms with the situations of danger or deprivation he or she must face. The key to dealing with anxiety consists in having advance information about the scope of the threat so that one can do some initial spadework to avert a full-blown crisis.

When anxiety is excessive and becomes overblown, it can be crippling and destructive. Someone with a high anxiety level often feels as though he or she were living under a dark cloud all the time, and gradually the unresolved conflicts churning within wear the person down. He or she is often extremely tense and restless and at times unable to explain his or her feelings or behavior. Usually such a person shows extreme and increasing caution in interpersonal relationships and creates more distance by rationalizing, "I've been burned once.

I don't want to risk the pain of being burned again." So the person withdraws farther into himself or herself, and the cycle of self-defeating behavior draws in tighter.

A moderate level of anxiety can be a catalyst for taking positive steps to alter a seemingly negative situation, to get moving again and begin to deal with one's personal agenda. There is a curious ring to the prayer that follows the Lord's Prayer in the Roman liturgy, when the priest prays: " . . . protect us from all anxiety, as we wait in joyful hope for the coming of our Savior, Jesus Christ." When one recognizes that a certain amount of anxiety can prompt real growth and change in relationships, the occasional priestly interjection of "protect us from all *needless* anxiety" makes better sense. However, the positive or negative value of anxiety is a matter of degree; if anxiety climbs to a neurotic level, it can compound an already sagging sense of self-worth, exaggerate the perceived loss, and funnel into a more dangerous, self-defeating pattern of behavior, depression.

Like anxiety, *depression* is a normal part of any mourning process and exists in two degrees: acute (temporary) and chronic (habitual). Depression is brought on when a person's sense of security is threatened over a loss or the perceived danger of loss of a valued person or thing. In coming to terms with such a loss or separation, people often find themselves unable to grieve openly, to talk out their feelings and release what is pent up within. While depression is usually triggered by an external event, internally it brings with it lowered feelings of self-worth and heightened feelings of guilt and resentment.

Classically, the definition of depression is "anger turned inward," though a more useful understanding may be sought from the following formula: depression = feelings of inferiority + anger x self-pity. We have already seen that each of these factors is a typical offshoot of a crisis of loss, in particular the loss of a spouse, but the combination of these elements in large doses can be debilitating and at times even lethal (the full-blown extension of depression is suicide).

Depression is generally marked with feelings of sadness, helplessness, and a devalued self-image, all related in some way to an actual or threatened loss. Much negative fallout accompanies depression, and it is manifested in a variety of physical, emotional, and psychological ways. Self-confidence and self-esteem nose-dive. Anger churns beneath the surface while the persons feel unloved, forgotten, abandoned. There is a tendency to brood over past injuries and become trapped in a revolving door of unresolved negative feelings, especially anger and guilt. Along with having distorted images of past and present relationships, depressed persons typically exhibit bristling self-defense mechanisms to keep others at a distance, while they drop into the rut of resisting change and settling into a secure pattern of relating to others. They become narcissistic, essentially preoccupied with self, while at the same time they expend enormous amounts of time and energy concealing certain aspects of themselves, such as their deep-seated negative feelings.

Gradually this pattern wears the person down, and his or her pace slows. Drive and motivation wane. He or she craves attention yet somehow refuses to make the effort to extend the self and to respond in a relationship. Massive dependencies can begin to crop up at this point. The capacity for self-inflicted pain escalates and is reflected in a variety of ways such as accident-proneness. The sufferer often resorts to sarcasm, stressing the weaknesses of another to avoid dealing with his or her own. Frequently, the person has diminished interest in his or her job and finds it hard to concentrate. He or she often becomes apathetic, irritable, bored, poorly motivated, rigid, and withdrawn, and frequently derives little or no enjoyment from recreation or peer relationships.

Depression is a consuming result of unresolved feelings released in the aftermath of a crisis of loss. It has many serious physical side-effects that tend to affect different persons in varied ways: loss of appetite/overeating, oversleeping/insomnia, general fatigue, headaches and backaches, stomach ailments, and a host of other problems. Depression is marked by severe mood changes, especially funneling into gloominess and sadness as the person withdraws further into himself or herself and becomes more indifferent to others, no longer caring about what is happening in his or her life. At times these feelings can verge on self-punishment and masochism, as when a soldier who receives a "Dear John" letter impulsively volunteers to "take the point" in a night patrol or head up a "suicide squadron." In *extreme* cases, on top of this lack of concern for personal safety and preoccupation with self-destruction, depressed persons often develop an addictive reliance on drugs or alcohol as a means of seeking release from the feelings of loss or failure. In extreme cases the danger of suicide may be present; if so, one should seek professional help.

Anger is a potentially explosive and thinly veiled element of depression; it is basically a response to a perceived threat or hurt or to the frustration of not getting what one wants. In some ways anger is less of a feeling than a vehicle and a screen for handling fear. It can take a number of forms in different individuals, such as frustration, resentment, defiance, and indignation.

Though a "negative" emotion, anger can be a positive value and can help a person cope with a threatening situation. Like fear, anger is a response to a perceived danger to one's well-being, and when moderate it serves a very useful protective function. Too much or too little anger, however, can compromise an individual's effectiveness in relationships. A person who does not assert his or her feelings can be easily written off or taken advantage of, while one who is too assertive can overpower or scare away those in his or her path.

Anger is obviously a potent force that should be dealt with directly and constructively, not bottled up or repressed. As children, many Christians learned that anger was a "cardinal sin" to be scrupulously avoided. Part of the upshot of that narrow approach is that since many people were conditioned never to deal directly with negative feelings in relationships, they became passive-aggressive in their dealings with others, smiling on the surface while seething with anger within.

The model of Jesus encountered in the Gospels is a good counterpoint in this regard. The Greek word that the Bible often uses to describe Jesus, and which is usually translated into English as "moved to compassion" or "moved to pity" really means "to feel deeply, in the gut and in the bowels, both love and anger." That Jesus felt things deeply and expressed both love and anger is clearly expressed throughout the Gospels. Jesus could be moved to righteous indignation, as in the familiar scene of casting the moneychangers out of the Temple, or in the Marcan account of Peter's profession of faith at Caesarea Philippi, where Jesus remonstrates with Peter for wanting to have him on his own terms, and says to the rock on which he will build his Church, "Get behind me, you Adversary!" One need only read the twenty-third chapter of the Gospel of Matthew to see that in the Evangelist's view Jesus was capable of expressing strong negative feelings, in lambasting some of the scribes and Pharisees as hypocrites: " . . . you viper's nest . . . , you whitewashed tombs . . . , you strain out the gnat and swallow the camel. . . ." Contrary to some of the prevailing images of Christian piety, Jesus cannot be reduced to a pale, meek Galilean but was a man of deep feelings and personal convictions, willing to express them openly and appropriately when necessary—a model worthy of imitation.

The Christian needs to remember that anger is not of itself a sin. The Apostle Paul touches on this point in his letter to the Ephesians: "If you are angry, let it be without sin. The sun must not go down on your wrath; do not give the devil a chance to work on you. . . . In place of these, be kind to one another, compassionate, and mutually forgiving, just as God has forgiven you in Christ" (4:26-27,32). Anger itself is not sinful, although, in the old catechism jargon, it can be an "occasion of sin" if it isolates one from others and forces one to turn in on oneself and against or away from others. That kind of isolation is the very essence of sin. But anger can be an "occasion of grace" as well, an opportunity and a catalyst for growth if the person is open to channeling constructively the energy it brings.

Guilt is a feeling of blameworthiness that a person often puts on himself or herself in association with the feeling that he or she has done something wrong. Guilt is always present to some degree in acute grieving. Following the end of a marriage, when deep feelings of attachment are set free, it tends to surface quickly.

After the tragic Coconut Grove nightclub fire in Boston in 1942, psychologist Erich Lindemann began a groundbreaking study of the survivors and of the victims' families. He found a strong degree of guilt present in all of the interviewees and observed that if the survivors were to work through such an overload of feelings, they first needed to recognize and accept the fact of the loss and its accompanying pain, and struggle to come in touch with the dimensions of the now-severed relationship. To do this, they had to review past activities and experiences shared with the deceased and ultimately come to the realization that they must adjust the various aspects of their new life in order to cope without the presence of the now-departed loved one.

Feeling guilty is a normal, healthy part of the grieving process. It can be complicated, however, by a low self-image, a lack of willingness to offer or accept forgiveness, remorse for marital infidelity or for having initiated the separation or divorce, or by giving in to such escapist tendencies as compulsive drinking, gambling, drugs, or workaholism. If a person does not deal appropriately with his or her guilt feelings after the end of a marriage, they can become overblown and immobilizing. In order to be able to work through feelings of guilt constructively, it is first necessary to recognize the finality of the lost relationship or object. Then one must seek out others who will give comfort and support and be good listeners as one verbalizes some of the deep-seated feelings of hostility and guilt.

Traditionally, many Catholics have had an unhealthy sense of guilt, typified in the "number and species," laundry-list approach to sin—an approach encouraged by the old catechisms. If a person is conditioned to think that harboring angry feelings and thoughts is abnormal, sinful, or otherwise unacceptable, this may prompt excessive guilt feelings. Such angry feelings need to be talked through in a relationship, since things that are felt to be "unspeakable" tend to engender far more guilt than those expressed openly.

Feelings of guilt, like all other feelings, are unhealthy only if they are present in an excessive and self-defeating way. Normal, healthy, concerned persons feel guilt (only sociopaths don't). We can expect that people will suffer in any genuine crisis of loss. In fact, many counselors feel there is something wrong with a spouse who does *not* experience a sense of guilt about the end of the marriage. Such a spouse, they say, can hardly have any serious understanding of or concern about the harm that a breakup can cause to both partners and to any children involved. To put it bluntly, if a person does not feel guilty after the end of a marriage, it is doubtful that he or she invested significantly in the relationship. But if the survivor gets in touch with the feelings stirred up by the marriage's end, refuses to fall prey to the "blame game," and begins to take responsibility for the directions his or her life will now be assuming, he or she is probably well on the way to emotional recovery.

The final feeling to consider in our look at emotional adjustment following the end of a marriage is *loneliness*. Loneliness springs from the sense of loss triggered by the separation. Most people tend to underestimate their own inner resources and feel that their emotional survival rests more on others than on themselves. While emotional recovery clearly depends on both oneself and others, the more important element is really the survivor's ability to use the pain of the situation as a means of growing and of coming to a renewed and stronger sense of self.

If a person lacks a secure sense of self, then the onset of loneliness prompted by the end of a marriage may seem to be a kind of death, since he or she has lost so much that was dear. There is no longer a warm body for companionship in bed and to make love to, no longer another adult in the household for small talk or even for fighting. Since there is no longer a significant other to share one's feelings and concerns, daily tasks and routines tend to lose their meaning, and one can become increasingly lethargic, bored, and unable to manage one's time and energy well.

Even in the most oppressive marriage situations, often a certain measure of security and stability offers a clear sense of identity and prevents loneliness. After the end of a marriage, all members of the family (the custodial parent, the absent parent, and the children) discover that ties with others have been significantly disrupted and that past friendships can wane. As a result, they find themselves more and more distant, alienated, and withdrawn from others. Socially, they may come to feel like pariahs, misfits, outcasts. These feelings may be especially strong during holiday seasons, when unresolved feelings from the past are kicked up; people who cannot enter into the spirit of the season feel that they are scrooge-like, heartless, rejecting and rejected.

The only way to confront such feelings head-on and to deal with them is to rebuild one's sense of confidence and esteem. To do that, one must reach out to old friends and acquaintances for support and must get in touch with family members who are willing to stand by in time of need. Sometimes, ironically, new friends and acquaintances will emerge to offer support. So joining clubs or groups can help one reduce feelings of isolation and alienation and can give a sense of comfort and consolation as one realizes that others have been through the same experience or are now in the same boat.

Now that we have sketched out some of the dimensions of anxiety, depression, anger, guilt, and loneliness, it will be valuable to examine briefly some ways of coming to terms with these feelings. There are certain specific steps a person can take while on the road to recovery. These almost always involve reinvesting in relationships, constructively channeling energy, reestablishing one's independent identity, and remaining open to new experiences. In the recovery process, a great connection exists between the person's regaining a sense of competency and self-esteem and his or her emotional recovery and healthy adjustment. Obviously, the first thing called for is to recognize the true dimensions of the loss. Then the person must seek to satisfy his or her personal needs in a positive vein and to reestablish interaction in relationships.

Every person has deep needs to belong, to have definite measure of control over his or her destiny, and to receive and offer affection. Every person wants to feel important, capable, and lovable. If in the aftermath of a crisis of loss in marriage someone can establish mutuality of interest, trust, and love in a relationship, then he or she will be far better able to draw on inner resources in order to risk again in a bond of love. To be sure, the end of a marriage is an unwelcome interruption in any life. But it can serve as an opportunity for authentic growth if the persons involved commit themselves to come to terms with the past, recognize self-defeating behavior, and work to change it. Unless this happens, prospects for making it in any intimate relationship, especially in a second marriage, are dim.

Part Two

EXPLORING SOME
RELIGIOUS ISSUES

4

THE NATURE OF CHRISTIAN MARRIAGE

The most all-embracing relationship that binds men and women together is marriage. More than any other human bond, marriage touches both parties in all their dimensions. For the Christian, marriage is an offshoot of creation, a gift of God from the beginning that is both a human reality and a saving mystery—a human reality with clear religious overtones.

The vision of marriage presented in the first book of the Bible stresses that God willed that human persons find their fulfillment in relationships with others: "It is not good for the man to be alone. I will make a suitable partner for him" (Genesis 2:18). The various phrases used in the Genesis account to describe the creation of Adam and Eve form an eloquent summary of the biblical vision of marriage as a total sharing of husband and wife: "partner," "two in one flesh," "bone of my bones and flesh of my flesh."

Already in the Hebrew Bible, marriage was viewed as an image of the covenant between God and the people of Israel. The God of Israel made himself present to his people through a promise of love and fidelity; the faithful and enduring bond between spouses was viewed as an earthly sign of that divine covenant. On the basis of these biblical insights, marriage came to be recognized first and foremost as a personal, mutual commitment between a woman and a man in which the main values witnessed to were enduring love and faithfulness and a willingness both to offer and to seek forgiveness and recon-ciliation in broken relationships.

In reality, Jesus did not create a sacramental sign proper to marriage; rather, he built on what already existed and restored its original God-intended dimensions, to be lived in the union of two in one flesh. Christian marriage took as its model the example of Jesus' own life and love and his faithfulness to the Church. In Christian marriage, creation, the covenant, and redemption are intertwined. Jesus is seen as the bridegroom; his bride is the Church. Jesus, who loves, redeems, and cares for his people, is offered as a model and guide for spouses in their marital relationships. When marriage is seen from this perspective, it can be said that what was inherently present in human marriage from the beginning could become clearer and find expression in the vision of Jesus and could reach its full-ness when witnessed in the context of a faith community.

It is no accident that John's Gospel used a wedding feast as the setting for the first sign in which Jesus manifested his saving power, since for most Christians, marriage is the primary and most effective means of channeling grace and salvation. In his letter to the Ephesians, Paul expounded on the connection between the self-giving love of Jesus and marital love: "Hus-bands, love your wives, as Christ loved the church. He gave himself up for her. . . . Husbands should love their wives as they do their own bodies. He who loves his wife loves himself" (5:25-28). The author of the letter to the Hebrews expressed a general Christian teaching when he wrote, "Let marriage be honored in every way . . ." (13:4). For the early Christians, the importance of the covenant relationship in marriage is demonstrated most clearly in the unqualified injunction of Mat-thew's Gospel: "Let no man separate what God has joined" (19:6). While based on the Jewish tradition of the books of Genesis and Tobit and the witness of the prophets, such as Malachi and Jeremiah, the Christian understanding of marriage as an expression of personal, faithful, and fruitful love not only reflects dimensions already present in human marriage, but viewed in light of Jesus' vision of the Kingdom of God allows for the possibility of a fuller realization of these human-Christian values.

Traditionally, Catholics have spoken of marriage as a sacrament, a sign of something made holy. A sacrament is a meeting point, an encounter with another person, or a moment in which one is nourished and challenged to grow in a deeper realization of God's presence and grace acting in the world. When St. Augustine first applied the term *sacrament* to marriage, he likened human marriage to the permanent and indissoluble union of Christ and the Church, a faithful and permanent bond of love. A sacrament, for Augustine, was an "outward sign of an inner grace," which both contains in itself and brings about what it signifies. In marriage, the love that binds a husband and wife together is a living sign that makes the reality of God's love and faithfulness present in the world. Today, the focus in Christian marriage is personal and relational, with mutual love, faithfulness, and endurance as its outward signs. As each partner strives to "make flesh" for the other the self-giving love of Christ, each is capable of sanctifying and enriching the other for a lifetime.

Because Christian marriage is a powerful symbol that represents Christ in the world, the church leaders at the Second Vatican Council referred to marriage and family life as a "domestic church." Vatican II's *Pastoral Constitution on the Church in the Modern World* depicted marriage as "an intimate partnership," a "communion of life and love," "the mutual gift of two persons," a "conjugal covenant." That document envisioned the principal end of marriage as "the determined effort to perfect each other through the mutual interchange and sharing of life as a whole."

The same document captured the truest meaning of the sacrament of marriage:

> A man and a woman, who by the marriage covenant of conjugal love "are no longer two, but one flesh" (Matthew 19:6), render mutual help and service to each other through an intimate union of their persons and of their actions. Through this union they experience the meaning of their oneness and attain to it with growing perfection day by day. As a mutual gift of two persons, this intimate union, as well as the good of the children,

imposes total fidelity on the spouses and argues for an unbreakable oneness between them.

Christ the Lord abundantly blessed this many-faceted love, welling up as it does from the fountain of divine love and structured as it is on the model of His union with the Church. For as God of old made Himself present to His people through a covenant of love and fidelity, so now the Savior of men and the Spouse of the Church comes into the lives of married Christians through the sacrament of matrimony. He abides with them thereafter so that, just as He loved the Church and handed Himself over on her behalf, the spouses may love each other with perpetual fidelity through mutual self-bestowal.

Authentic married love is caught up into divine love and is governed and enriched by Christ's redeeming power. . . . (no. 48)

To put it simply, the marriage of Christians is both a human reality and a sacred mystery, raised by Christ and his Church to the dignity of a sacrament.

5

BIBLICAL APPROACHES
TO DIVORCE AND REMARRIAGE

The prevailing Jewish attitudes toward divorce prior to the time of Christ may be found in one of the first books of the Law: Deuteronomy, Chapters 22 and 24. To state it briefly, the Law of Moses allowed a marriage to be dissolved on the grounds of adultery (Deuteronomy 22:22) or of "something indecent" (24:1-4), though in the course of time the latter grounds came to be understood in two distinctly different manners by the rival rabbinic schools. Some, under the leadership of Rabbi Shammai, saw the grounds for divorce as consisting solely in adultery, while others, under the banner of Rabbi Hillel, held that a man could divorce his wife for any perceived failure, including burning the porridge for the evening meal! In contrast to Roman law, divorce among the Jews could be initiated only by a man, never by a woman. The sexist inequity of this attitude is illustrated in the writings of the Jewish historian Josephus, in *The Antiquities*: "For it is only the man who is permitted to do this [dissolve a marriage], and not even a divorced woman may marry again on her own initiative without her former husband's consent." It should be pointed out, however, that the Mosaic law sought to prevent the woman from being arbitrarily dismissed, and her husband had to present to the elders a writ justifying his action. Unfortunately, no matter how intolerable the marital situation may have been, Jewish law granted the woman no such recourse.

While certain concessions were taken into consideration on account of human frailty, throughout the unfolding course of the Hebrew Bible a growing view held that according to God's will the marriage covenant between two believers should be irrevocable. The prophets of Israel began to include the idea of faithfulness to one's wife as a part of the covenant morality to which each devout Jew was called, nowhere seen more clearly than in the book of the Prophet Malachi:

> Has not the one God created us?
> Why then do we break faith with each other,
>> violating the covenant of our fathers?
>> . . . the Lord is witness
>> between you and the wife of your youth,
> With whom you have broken faith,
>> though she is your companion, your betrothed wife.
> Did he not make one being, with flesh and spirit? . . .
> You must then safeguard life that is your own,
>> and not break faith with the wife of your youth.
> For I hate divorce,
>> says the Lord, the God of Israel. . . .
>> (Malachi 2:10,14-16)

Jesus followed in this tradition when he rejected outright the interpretations that made divorce a legal fiat of the husband against his wife, and it is against this background that the clear departure of Jesus' teaching on the permanency of marriage must be understood. The message of Jesus on the indissolubility of marriage is a radical, certain, and unqualified thrust of his ethical teaching and a sharp break with the Law of Moses. The call to permanence that he unconditionally issued to his followers seemed to catch them off guard by the totality of its demands. It is a hard saying, bound up in the cost of discipleship.

In Mark's Gospel (10:2-9, paralleled in Matthew 19:3-9), the evangelist lays out the basis for Jesus' teaching. For Mark, this instruction gave the followers of Jesus such a jolt that it had to be repeated within the confines of the home of one of them so they could be sure that they had heard properly: "Whoever divorces his wife and marries another commits adultery against her; and the woman who divorces her husband and marries another commits adultery" (Mark 10:12).

There are a number of noteworthy features here. First, Mark, writing in a Roman context, takes into account the provisions of Roman law that allowed a woman as well as a man to initiate divorce proceedings, and Mark uniformly applies the teaching of Jesus to both sexes alike, thereby raising the status of woman. Here, Jesus asserted that in the time of Moses divorce was permitted because of the hardness of people's hearts, that is, human sinfulnesss. But Jesus went on to undertake a collision course with the Mosaic law when he changed the question from what is *permissible* to what is *willed by God* in the order of creation. For Jesus, the essence of marriage was found in God's initial plan of creation, spelled out in the earliest chapters of Genesis: Jesus said, "At the beginning of creation God made them male and female; for this reason a man shall leave his father and mother and the two shall become as one. They are no longer two but one flesh. Therefore let no one separate what God has joined" (Mark 10:6-9). For Jesus, divorce was a sin, in the root biblical sense of the word: a falling short, missing the mark, not measuring up to the sought-after goal. He did not hedge on the call to permanence in marriage. Any response short of a radical obedience to this directive could be viewed as less than ideal in the eyes of God, an action for which the responsible parties might stand in need of healing and forgiveness. Mark sums up Jesus' teaching and then makes it fully explicit as if to express a fundamental law for the disciples in their preaching. The thrust of this message found in Mark, the earliest of the four Gospels, finds echoes in the others as well.

Luke draws on an early source of sayings of the Lord to state, without qualification: "Everyone who divorces his wife and marries another commits adultery. The man who marries a woman divorced from her husband likewise commits adultery" (16:18). While Matthew draws on this same source in his Gospel in the section we call the Sermon on the Mount, he modifies it somewhat to say, "It was also said, 'Whenever a man divorces his wife, he must give her a decree of divorce.' What I say to you is: everyone who divorces his wife—lewd conduct is a separate case—forces her to commit adultery. The man who marries a divorced woman likewise commits adultery" (5:31-32).

This earlier saying is linked in Matthew's Gospel to a passage that takes as its point of departure the sayings of Jesus on divorce in Mark. In Matthew 19:3-9, the evangelist introduces an exceptive clause permitting divorce on the grounds of the wife's unchastity, which some interpret as adulterous conduct (as a consistent style of life), following the tradition of the strictest teachers of the Law from the Shammai school. Matthew presumes the possibility of divorce on the grounds of such "lewd conduct," since in his view such actions have already of themselves irrevocably severed the covenant bond of marriage. Matthew put it this way: "I now say to you, whoever divorces his wife (lewd conduct is a separate case) and marries a divorced woman commits adultery" (19:9). While it is clear that Matthew retains a forceful rejection of divorce based on the Genesis texts, his exceptive clause does allow for divorce on the grounds of adulterous conduct. Many biblical scholars today feel that Mark would have implicitly understood *adultery* as grounds for divorce, in view of Deuteronomy 22:22 and 24:1-4; in this case the notable exceptive clauses of Matthew would be consistent with Mark's earlier teaching. In any event, it is difficult to find unequivocal evidence in the Scriptures for imposing an absolute rule of indissolubility, though no serious reader would dispute that Jesus clearly presented it as an ideal for all Christians to strive after.

Some prefer to see the exceptive clauses of Matthew as an attempt by the early Church to soften the demands and claims made by Jesus on his community of followers and as a concession to human weakness and sinfulness. It is certain that Jesus' teaching on indissolubility does constitute a moral imperative for every married couple, without exception, to seek for, and symbolizes the ideal union of husband and wife. But contemporary Scripture scholars and moral theologians are increasingly recognizing that in addition to the ideal moral imperative that Jesus issued, the circumstances and details of a particular situation need to be taken into account in order to avoid excessive and inhumane legalism. There is no doubt that the injunction of Christ and of his Church to give witness to the ideal of faithfulness and permanence in marriage will be preached and adhered to in every age. But as even the young and zealous early Christian communities discovered for themselves, certain adaptations and concessions may have to be made as a sign of compassion and mercy and for the sake of observing the supreme law, the care of souls.

A further example of this sort of pastoral accommodation is found in Paul. In his first letter to the church at Corinth, the Apostle plainly repudiated the practice of divorce (1 Corinthians 7:10-11). But while he saw marital permanence as the ideal, Paul did not conceive of it as an absolute that would brook no exceptions. The particular situation that Paul faced was a marriage between a believer and a nonbeliever. The bottom line of Paul's concern was to maintain a measure of peace that would reach out and touch all facets of the couple's lives and have its impact on every level of the most basic human relationship of marriage. On this basis, Paul came to the conclusion that if the nonbeliever refused to respect the faith and conscience of the believer and as a result helped make any further mutual, free expression of conscience impossible, then the believer could be declared absolved of the marital bond.

On the basis of the biblical evidence we can conclude that Jesus' teaching on marriage and divorce served to elevate the status of woman; it removed the question from a purely legal ground and placed it within the context of God's plan for all creation; it expressed a radical and uncompromising demand that every believer strive to live out a permanent, faithful union in marriage; and finally, it recognized that there may be some grounds for dissolving the marital bond if sinful behavior has made it impossible to achieve the ideal he had set out. There is no doubt that Jesus' ethical teaching on marital indissolubility and permanence was a sharp departure from the prevailing customs of the Jewish religion and of Roman society. But even before the ink had dried on the last Gospel, the early Christian communities came to realize the struggles and the tension between the "now" and the "not yet," the still-unrealized totality of the values and ideals of the Kingdom of God, and the inroads caused by a sinful world. The writings of both Matthew and Paul, while remaining faithful to the vision of Jesus, sought to accommodate to the needs of their church members who had fallen short or missed the mark on the matter of marital permanence. Their ministries of healing and reconciliation might well serve as a model for our churches today.

6

IS MARRIAGE FOREVER?

It was Jesus who first clearly expressed the Christian view that marriage was intended by God to be permanent, and the Catholic Church has always retained this value and set it before its members as the ideal. The official teaching of the Catholic Church on marital indissolubility is that once a marriage is validly witnessed in a ceremony and consummated physically it may not be dissolved by any human power, either by one of the partners or by any other individual, without recourse to the proper church authority. In this view, the marriage bond may ordinarily be dissolved only by the death of one of the partners. In spite of the erosion that contemporary social structures have foisted upon marital stability, especially in the industrialized West, the Church continues to give witness to this ideal, in the belief that it is intended by God and is humanly realizable by those seeking to achieve it.

The most basic understanding of this approach to Christian marriage views a man and a woman as committing themselves to each other for their whole lives, in a total, unconditional, mutual gift of self. This authentic and permanent expression of love is offered for the good of the spouses as well as of their children and of society at large. For this reason Christ established the general principle and moral directive that God intends all marriages to be indissoluble.

But even certain of the biblical witnesses who vigorously upheld the Church's teaching on marital permanency, such as Paul and Matthew, allowed for exceptions to this norm in the lived realities of their communities in order to extend a measure of mercy and compassion to those who suffered irrevocable marital failure. And at various times and places the Catholic Church has allowed for further exceptions. It is important to realize that many of the factors that threaten the stability of marriage today were unknown to the apostolic Church, and some of these factors are prompting a reexamination of certain aspects of church discipline and sacramental practice that we will consider in detail elsewhere in this book. While few in the Christian community today would seriously question the value of upholding the ideal norm of indissolubility, many are looking for a pastoral approach to the needs of divorced and remarried Catholics that will respond better to human realities and be attentive to the pastoral situations that have arisen in recent decades.

A look at history reveals that the great early church thinkers were split on the question of divorce and remarriage within a church context. Such noted ancient Christian writers as St. Basil and St. Cyril permitted remarriage in the belief that for the good of the souls involved it was best to allow it on limited grounds and with certain proportionate reasons. Some early bishops prescribed penances before readmission to the sacraments, especially for the person who was deemed primarily responsible for the breakdown of the marriage. While an innocent party was allowed to remarry, it was considered more praiseworthy to remain single. Until the eighth century, in many places the Church permitted remarriage in the case of adultery, desertion, or the abduction of a spouse with little prospect for return. In each of these contexts, the underlying principle was clear. Remarriage was not seen as a part of God's plan for creation, but if in fact a marriage had come apart, this sad fact could be recognized and remarriage tolerated, though not outrightly encouraged.

In speaking of a person who had remarried for "a valid motive," an early church Father wrote, "The divine word does not condemn him nor exclude him from the church or its common life; but she tolerates it rather on account of his weakness." St. Cyril, writing with an eye on the famous exceptive clause of Matthew 19:6, added: "God, as I finally believe, adapted his laws to the measure of human nature," that is, made concessions to the limitations of human nature and sinfulness. The Irish monks invoked this same concept in the fifth, sixth, and seventh centuries to temper the harsh impact of the laws of indissolubility when strictly and universally applied.

Both in the Christian East and West the ideal of the indissolubility of marriage has always been recognized. Nevertheless, aware of the painful fact that Christian ideals are not always humanly attainable, and with regret and sufficient restrictions to confine the practice to serious cases, history tells us that the Christian Church has constantly accepted divorce and remarriage in the East and tolerated it for more than a thousand years in the Latin West, at least in certain places and at certain times. A profound shift in the Roman Catholic practice occurred in the late twelfth and early thirteenth centuries, when the primacy of church law (and the accompanying juridical, and at times legalistic, mindset) took hold, though in the East the old practice remained undisturbed. Some theologians stress that there is a validity to each of these divergent approaches to the pastoral treatment of divorced and remarried persons even though the Eastern approach today seems a more practical pastoral solution, as we will see in the following chapter.

The more rigoristic posture that took root in the West and filtered down to the present day in Roman Catholicism was very hard on many who fell short of the ideal of indissolubility, particularly those who remarried. Their deep sense of personal failure was further compounded by denial of access to the Eucharist or by excommunication, which deprived them of church status and their right to certain sacraments. Unfortunately, those who did not measure up to the ideal were often made to feel that they had committed an "unforgivable sin" and could have no real hope of forgiveness. Recent modifications in pastoral practice have altered this perspective, and these will be considered in this book in the sections on excommunication, access to the Eucharist, the internal forum solution; and the annulment process. Many of the practical difficulties that Catholics in broken marriages experienced were the residue of an older, ends-oriented, and narrowly physical approach which saw marriage's full consummation in a biological act but had little regard for the quality of human relationships. This older approach prompted the great Protestant theologian Karl Barth to remark that Catholics had no theology of marriage, but only of the marriage ceremony and of the first night. To a large extent, this approach was not corrected until the Second Vatican Council in the middle 1960s.

It is interesting to note, however, that in its tradition and in contemporary pastoral practice the Church officially allows divorced persons in second unions to continue living together, provided that they do so as "brother and sister" (i.e., abstain from sexual intercourse); otherwise they must not receive the Eucharist. Even under this official posture, the Church encourages and even obliges these persons to attend Sunday Mass and admits that they can live Christianly and humanly in a second marriage in all things but genital sexual expression, and that they have no real obligation to renounce the present union on account of the former marriage, which practically speaking no longer exists. Apart from excessively emphasizing genitality and officially restricting access to the Eucharist (more will be said on this point later in this book), the present pastoral practice of the Roman Catholic Church does not in reality differ very much from the Orthodox "principle of economy," though the Western Church's theological and pastoral bases are considerably less pliant. To adopt a more tolerant attitude toward second marriages, a là the Orthodox, would in reality be no more inconsistent with the principle of indissolubility than certain current practices within Roman Catholicism are.

For a pilgrim people living in a world where grace and sin are intermingled, the more rigid and legalistic approach that Roman Catholicism assumed during the High Middle Ages leaves itself open to many hard questions and much theological and pastoral review in the face of contemporary realities. Or, as one North American bishop, Archbishop Henri Legare of Canada, remarked in an intervention at the World Synod of

Bishops meeting on family ministry in 1980 (*Origins*, vol. 10, no. 18, Oct. 16, 1980, p. 281): "Reexamination of doctrine on the sacrament of marriage is thus made necessary by the application of a ministry of mercy without denying the evangelical demand for conjugal fidelity. Indissolubility is maintained. But would it not be possible to propose a pastoral approach that is more attentive to the situation that faces us?" That is *the* question.

7

THE ORTHODOX
"PRINCIPLE OF ECONOMY"

In recent years, Roman Catholic attitudes and pastoral practice toward persons in failed marriages have undergone significant revision. It is helpful to look to the practice of the Eastern Churches in this matter, since their communion with Rome was described by Pope Paul VI as "almost perfect." The Orthodox have a long-established marital discipline that permits remarriage in church following divorce on the basis of the "principle of *economy*." In the root sense of the word in Greek, *economy* means managing a household or private affairs. In this usage, as Webster notes, it means "the efficent and sparing use of the means available for the end proposed." Economy suggests the concept of stewardship, of management on another's behalf. It acquired further meaning in the religious context: in the administration of penance and arrangement of a sinner's reconciliation with the Church; as a suspension of the strict administration of the Church's legal or disciplinary norms (in a way similar to the Roman Catholic notion of "dispensation"); and as an application of the sacraments in a merciful way in the Orthodox Church.

The practice of economy has been the uninterrupted custom of the Eastern Churches and the frequent practice in the West, over the course of many centuries. While the Christian churches have always considered divorce a tragedy and a consequence of human sinfulness, the Orthodox have shown a willingness to forgive the guilt of the spouses in a broken marriage, providing they show repentance for any sinful actions that contributed to the failure of the marriage. The Orthodox Church does not claim the power to grant divorces or to dissolve marriages, but just as it joyfully witnesses the beginning of sacramental marriages, so too it concedes sadly that some of these unions may die. The Orthodox position holds that marriage can cease to be a true sacramental sign when the union is severed through sin, selfishness, and the absence of the essential elements of faith and love.

This understanding is reflected in *The Orthodox-Roman Catholic "Agreed Statement on the Sanctity of Marriage"* issued in 1978, which states that although the Eastern Orthodox Church holds to the ideal of marital permanence, " . . . out of consideration of the human realities, (it) permits divorce . . . and tolerates remarriages in order to avoid further human tragedies." The principle of economy maintains two vital strands of the Christian tradition: the God-intended ideal of indissolubility in Christian marriage, and the possibility of pastoral accommodation in tolerating certain remarriages when some unions fail. In a way similar to the Protestant notion of the tragic, this Orthodox stance is not to be seen as the endorsement of divorce, but rather as the practical acceptance and toleration of the reality that some marriages do in fact die. This position recognizes that while the Kingdom of God has already begun in the here and now, it has not yet been fully realized. Accordingly, despite the need to adhere faithfully to the call for Gospel perfection, one needs also to take into account the limitations and human sinfulness that at times squelch the possibility of attaining the fullness and perfection of Gospel values.

By invoking the principle of economy, the Orthodox Church seeks to head off even more dire consequences and holds out the possibility of a fresh start for those recovering from a spiritually disastrous marriage that for all intents and purposes is dead. After close examination by a priest, the Eastern Church may acknowledge formally that the previous marriage has been sapped of any spiritual foundation and destroyed by sin. From the Orthodox perspective, various grounds may obtain: plotting to murder the spouse; committing crimes carrying the death penalty; the occurrence of events whose consequences are the equivalent of natural death; adultery; insanity; sexual impotence; abandonment; and fraudulent or forced marriage.

In many of these situations, serious sanctions are imposed. Penances and fasting are enjoined on those who divorce (particularly upon the spouse more culpable for the breakup of the marriage), and a special, simplified penitential rite of marriage is used.

In short, Eastern practice regards remarriage following divorce as a pastoral opportunity to exercise a ministry of healing and reconciliation and to create the possibility of restoring the optimal goal of all persons involved: forming and maintaining an intimate union of life and love.

In this light, it would be incorrect to say that the Eastern Church "gives" divorces. Rather, it views divorce as a serious sin that cries out for a corrective and that seeks a new, healthy direction. So in its genuine pastoral concern, the Orthodox Church offers the victims of divorce the opportunity for repentance and a fresh beginning. It holds that sin and human frailty can and at times do erode the spiritual bonds of marriage and perhaps destroy them. In fact, this very theological stance prevailed in the West until the eleventh century. At that time a schism split the East from the West (1054), and the Roman Catholic Church acquired a more legalistic mindset that at times seemed to place law above the spiritual welfare of people.

The consistent belief and practice of the Eastern Church on divorce and remarriage has been that the marital bond can be severed for reasons other than natural death. While such breakdowns cause great pain and sadness, and while every reasonable attempt must be made to bring about a reconciliation, from this perspective the hard fact is that at times a marriage may actually cease to be a sacramental reality. Such an assessment should not be misconstrued either as a justification for divorce or as an attack on the value of indissolubility. Rather, it is a pastoral accommodation that realistically takes into account the sinful frailty of human nature. It is an *excep-*

tion to the rule of indissolubility, a concrete illustration of the kind of mercy and compassion that Jesus himself showed throughout his gospel ministry, and one which the communities of Matthew and Paul practiced as well.

For the Orthodox, the reality of an irreparably failed marriage is regretfully accepted. Remarriage with a church blessing may be sanctioned in order to stave off a greater harm, as we see in the conventional wisdom of Paul in his First Letter to the Corinthians: "It is better to marry than to be on fire" (7:9; cf. 1 Timothy 5:11-14). This long-standing tradition of the Eastern Church may have much to teach Roman Catholics. In fact, following the bishops' 1980 world synod on the family, Cardinal Joseph Ratzinger noted that the "Synod desired that a new and even more searching investigation—including even consideration of the praxis of the Eastern Church—be undertaken to make our pastoral compassion even more all-embracing." Because of the erosive forces in society that make long-term commitments to another person or way of life so difficult today, the need for this type of pastoral adaptation may be greater now than ever before.

The rightful concern of the bishops at the Synod was that the Church should serve as a sign of healing and merciful love in the world. The principle of economy was recognized by a number of the bishops as a powerful way of actualizing Christ's redemptive, healing love in the present context. Jesus came not for the holy but for sinners. He dined with tax collectors, prostitutes, and other known sinners. This kind of healing is the "household principle" of the Church and is the guiding force around which her practices and norms must be focused. The spirit and practice of the principle of economy is one way for this kind of healing love to take root in people's hearts in the present situation.

In reality, we must also conclude that there are weaknesses and deficiencies in the Orthodox approach, and at times it is even open to abuses. What is intended as a concession or a pastoral accommodation should be used cautiously and sparingly so that it does not obscure or ridicule the prevailing sense of Jesus' call to marital permanence. Otherwise, the ideal of indissolubility, though retained in theory, will degenerate and in practice be radically violated.

Though distinct from the Orthodox understanding, there are many values and advantages inherent in the Roman Catholic approaches described in the following chapters as the annulment process and the internal forum solution. Some Orthodox priests lament the nightmarish situations when they are called to help piece back together the lives of persons whose marriages have failed two or three times. They are at times inclined to feel that the Orthodox approach reaches too far in the other direction, making it possible for people to hurt themselves by entering a second or third union too facilely. A common Catholic question asked is, "Why does it take so long to get an annulment?" But one of the positive values of the Catholic approach is that it slows people down if they have a compulsion to remarry and allows them the time to get ready emotionally, spiritually, financially, and in a host of other ways, to assume the rights and obligations of a new union. At times the Roman Catholic approach is more successful in respecting the conscience judgments of the couple and in calling them to grow to a fuller experience of life and love. Often it is necessary to "put on the brakes" and allow a remarrying couple sufficient time to be sure that they are remarrying out of love and not out of need.

While couples stand to profit by studying the Orthodox practice of economy, the Roman Catholic teaching and discipline has an integrity and validity of its own. Yet the Orthodox stance may be showing us an equally valid and responsive path to seeking healing and wholeness in the aftermath of a spiritually disastrous marriage.

8

THE ANNULMENT PROCESS

To be truly sacramental, a marriage must contain within itself and be able to bring about what it signifies. In other words, it must both possess and form a union of life and love marked with the essential qualities of unity, fidelity, and indissolubility. Of late, the Christian community has been more ready to recognize that it is one thing to know about and desire marriage, but quite another thing to be able to actually bind oneself to a person in a lifelong, stable, heterosexual union. Today a number of elements are considered crucial to bringing about a valid sacramental marriage. The concern of the Church is that the partners enter into marriage deliberately and freely, with a solid intention and commitment to the values of permanence, faithfulness to each other, and openness to children.

For certain reasons, though, this type of union may have been precluded from the outset for a given couple. For instance, one of the partners may have been substantially in error about a basic quality of the other which, when discovered, gravely altered the life of the relationship. Or one person may not have made any authentic commitment to an exclusive, permanent union that is open to the gift of children. In short, some deficiency of will or of knowledge or of mental capacity may have prevented the couple from assuming and fulfilling the basic obligations of marriage. In any of these circumstances, the marriage may be judged to be null and void—that is, may never really have existed from the beginning. Roman Catholic church law recognizes more than thirty such criteria in treating cases of failed marriage in the external, public forum of the marriage tribunal (the marriage court) when it adjudicates what is commonly known as the annulment process. (In the following chapter, by contrast, we will discuss a non-juridical approach to annulment. That is, we will deal with the realm of conscience, not of law, when we discuss what is commonly known as the internal forum solution.)

An annulment is the formal declaration by the Catholic Church that in actual fact and in the eyes of church law a valid sacramental marriage never existed, in spite of appearances to the contrary. The practical upshot of a decree of nullity is the Church's declaration that both parties are no longer bound to that particular marriage relationship, since it has been determined that from the very beginning it lacked one or more of the elements essential to a valid union. An annulment does not assert that *no* real relationship ever existed, nor imply that the relationship was entered into with malice or any moral fault. Rather, by it the Church states that the relationship fell short and missed the mark of the intended properties of a sacramental marriage because it lacked at least one of the essential elements deemed necessary for such a union. Therefore it is no longer seen as a source of ongoing marital rights and obligations.

It is important to point out that a decree of nullity in no way brands as illegitimate children already born to the marriage, since prior to the annulment the union was presumed to be in good standing and to have enjoyed the Church's favor. All the annulment recognizes is that something essential was lacking from the start, so that it was, practically speaking, impossible for the couple to establish and maintain a permanent, loving Christian commitment. On this basis, the diocesan marriage tribunal may judge that the marriage in fact was not truly a sacramental union and need no longer be considered binding as a source of marital rights and obligations.

The past two decades have witnessed a revolution in the practice of marriage tribunals in the United States and throughout the world. In the early 1960s, only airtight nullity cases stood a chance of getting through the tribunals, if they were heard at all, and in most dioceses only one or two declarations of nullity were granted annually; even the great metropolitan sees seldom processed more than a dozen cases. From 1968, when 442 formal decisions were given in the United States (and not all of them affirmative), to 1981, when more than 35,000 affirmative decisions were granted, there has been an impressive overhaul of the annulment process.

There are two primary reasons for this pronounced change. For one, church courts began to implement new procedural norms that Pope Paul VI approved in 1970 for provisional use in the United States beginning in 1971. This new procedure allowed cases to be heard by a single judge rather than by a panel of three, and did away with the automatic review of affirmative decisions rendered; this vastly streamlined the time involved in the process. Secondly, church courts have increasingly used the insights of behavioral and social sciences to help clarify the essential meaning of marriage. This new way of gauging the sacramentality of a broken marriage was spotlighted recently, in a not altogether favorable way, by the late head of the Vatican's highest court, Cardinal Pericle Felici, who noted: "In some courts the number of nullity declarations on matrimony in the past ten years has increased notably, at times even reaching the astronomical figure of 5,000%." He went on to mention that the most common grounds proposed are "psychological immaturity and the incapacity to assume and fulfill conjugal responsibilities, especially with regard to the community of life and interpersonal relationships."

At times the Church recognizes that one or both partners may have failed to consent to sacramental marriage as the Church intends it, or that because of some psychological or sexual disorder they lack the capacity to assume and fulfill marital responsibilities. In point of fact, about 85% of all annulments presently granted in American tribunals are based on psychological grounds and recognize that one or both of the partners are unable to undertake fully and mutually sustain a sacramental marriage. Such a capacity may be lacking in the instances of emotional immaturity or pressured consent. Another common ground is the inability to create a permanent and mutual union of life and love on account of a serious mental, emotional, or sexual disorder. Recognizing and applying such grounds has offered tribunals a firm basis for rendering decisions that would have been unthinkable fifteen years ago. One noted American canonist, Father Thomas Green of the Catholic University of America, has called the application of psychological grounds for marriage nullity "the most significant jurisprudential development during the past decade."

In order to seek an annulment, after obtaining a civil divorce a petitioner may seek out a parish priest or contact a diocesan tribunal directly in order to probe the merits of the case and find out the local procedure. The person should be ready to discuss thoroughly the details of the broken marriage, including the family and personal background of each of the spouses; the relevant elements of the courtship, honeymoon, and marriage; the areas of tension and friction that marked the marital relationship; and the primary causes of the final breakup. Based on these discussions and other information obtained, an opinion is given as to whether there seems to be sufficient grounds for nullity—grounds that would warrant initiating the formal tribunal process. If so, the tribunal requires the testimony of several knowledgeable witnesses (preferably family members and friends with long-established relationships with both of the spouses) who are able to confirm the claims of the petitioners. All reasonable efforts are made to contact the other spouse to inform him or her of the proceeding and to solicit his or her input as well.

In general, under optimal conditions a case will be heard and acted on in less than a year from the time of filing with the tribunal, though it may take more or less time, depending upon the cooperation of the principals, the workload and efficiency of the tribunal members, and the nature of the case itself. There is a fee for the administrative costs incurred, which varies from diocese to diocese, though no petitioner should be turned away for lack of funds. In point of fact poverty is a major cause of marital breakdown, and many tribunals find that the bulk of the people they deal with are poor. In most diocesan tribunals and at the grassroots level in parishes, every reasonable effort will usually be made to help the petitioner prepare a suitable petition for annulment.

In spite of the many advances in tribunal procedure in recent years, and even taking into account the many ways that dedicated church lawyers and judges have served as healing instruments in a genuine ministry of reconciliation, sizable flaws remain in the system. An illustration of this is the fact that of the perhaps four million divorced and remarried Catholics in America, fewer than 2% have received annulments—a mere drop in the bucket. Even if every diocese in the country were able to boast a well-functioning tribunal with well-trained personnel and adequate resources (and recent survey data suggest that many do not), the fact remains that they are simply logistically incapable of handling, on anything less than a minuscule scale, the sheer numbers of persons affected. In addition, from the petitioner's perspective there are a number of less-than-desirable features to the annulment process. In some dioceses, the suggested fee for annulment would impose a serious financial strain on all but the most affluent. Some professional counselors are quick to assert that the process might as easily be a source of harm as of healing for their clients if it unnecessarily dredges up previously resolved negative feelings that could prove both painful and psychically damaging. Finally, some pastoral persons feel that the pendulum may have swung too far in recent years: that too much attention has been paid to the behavioral sciences at the expense of pastoral ministry, and that this has blunted the opportunities for pastoral intervention and follow-up.

There are other difficulties to contend with as well. A marked disparity exists in tribunal practice—for instance, in the case of the Archdiocese of New York and the neighboring Diocese of Brooklyn, where the contrast between the application of the same laws in their respective tribunals has been so pronounced as to be almost absurd. On the national scene, some tribunals are either non-functional or backward in their approaches; others have ceded enormous ground to psychology while perhaps losing perspective on the spiritual dimensions of the situation;

still others, however progressive, set such high fees that many persons are dissuaded from even attempting to file a case.

Finally, what about those divorced and remarried Catholics who do not appear to have any canonical grounds for annulment or who cannot produce sufficient evidence to support their case (which some estimate as high as 40% of the total number)? It is the right and the responsibility of every Catholic in a failed marriage to pursue the prospects of the external forum. But in truth, we must conclude that while for some it is a powerful means of achieving much healing and peace, for others it is little more than a dead end. For those who cannot present their case for consideration in the annulment process, however, a second option exists. It is discussed in the next chapter as the internal forum solution.

9

THE INTERNAL
FORUM SOLUTION

The last chapter considered the approaches to failed sacramental marriages in the Church's external forum, the marriage tribunal. In the annulment process and in all the canon law of marriage, the Church is concerned with embodying and promoting the human-Christian values that foster and maintain the good of individuals, the family, and society at large.

Yet laws and legal systems cannot offer specific solutions for every possible situation, and there are some distinct limitations that the external forum poses for those in broken marriages, as we have seen in discussing the annulment process. This fact was recognized in a 1973 report of the Canon Law Society of America: "The tribunal system in the United States is creaking. Even with the American Procedural Norms it does not meet the needs of so many American people. It is our conclusion that improving the present system is self-defeating." In fairness it must be said that serious efforts were made to improve the situation and that genuine advances were achieved in the ensuing decade. But it is also true that with the increased numbers of Catholics divorcing, even a well-functioning tribunal is frequently strapped in its attempts to respond adequately to the needs of petitioners, and formidable problems still plague the system.

A surprising percentage of American tribunals still have members with no advanced degree in canon law, and such persons may be largely ignorant of the profound advances in jurisprudence that have marked this field in the past twenty years. Many dioceses still have no full-time personnel assigned to tribunal work, and still more can boast only one full-time priest. Certain dioceses fail to meet the standards set by the *Code of Canon Law* itself, and, regrettably, few tribunals report that the support of their bishop is their greatest asset. Moreover, at times parish priests or tribunal staffs are simply too overwhelmed by their workloads to devote adequate attention to cases. Sometimes nullity cannot be established only because the validity of the first marriage cannot be disproved in the fashion prescribed by canonical and juridical procedure. In short, then, the present structure of diocesan marriage tribunals is often vastly inadequate to meet the needs of the sheer numbers of persons in failed marriages today.

Very few responsible Catholics would deny the positive value of law in safeguarding the integrity of marriage and family life and the ideal of indissolubility. But various situations exist that cannot be resolved satisfactorily by an external forum judgment, since the key facts may be known only in the intimacy of the marriage by the partners themselves. In such cases another legitimate pastoral option exists, known as the internal forum solution (I.F.S.).

The I.F.S. has a dual meaning. It refers to the manner whereby persons whose marriages are invalid according to the norms of canon law receive the sacraments publicly but in a way that keeps their irregular status hidden and does not cause scandal. It also refers to the way in which the decision is made to admit deserving couples to the sacraments. That is, the Catholic tradition views the I.F.S. as a private means of jurisdiction that requires consultation with a third party so that a couple and a pastoral guide may together arrive at an acceptable decision concerning the couple's status in the eyes of the Church. It is not simply the isolated decision of an individual. The process may be carried out in the internal forum of the sacrament of reconciliation (that is, in dialogue with a priest confessor), or it can happen in a non-sacramental context with another competent pastoral minister assisting the couple in the spiritual direction process.

The internal forum solution occurs in the private, hidden forum of conscience. Its hallmark is that it is primarily directed toward the immediate spiritual welfare of the parties involved, and takes place within the realm of their consciences. There are no cut-and-dried decisions within the internal forum: The process seeks to take into account the relevant factors and uniqueness of each particular case, since it is always necessary to tailor judgments individually when dealing with divorced and remarried persons or with those who are about to remarry.

The I.F.S. is a longstanding practice in the Roman Catholic Church, and it was affirmed in a letter to the heads of the national bishops' conferences from Cardinal Seper on behalf of the Vatican Congregation for the Doctrine of the Faith in 1973, where he wrote:

> In regard to the admission to the sacraments, the Ordinaries are asked on the one hand to stress the observance of the current discipline, and, on the other hand, to take care that the pastors of souls exercise special care to seek out those who are living in an irregular union by applying to the solution of such cases, in addition to other concrete means, the Church's approved practice in the internal forum.

Here, a key notion is that the prudent application of the I.F.S. belongs at the parish level. It is within the jurisdiction of the priest or other competent pastoral minister to help clarify and form the conscience decision of the couple and to assist in the process of spiritual direction and discernment so vital to the satisfactory application of the internal forum solution. The role of the pastoral minister is to help the couple arrive at their own conscience decision, rather than "giving them permission." It is also the weighty responsibility of the local pastoral ministers to educate the people to this practice. These ministers should be open, compassionate, and well apprised of the many and varied applications of the internal forum solution.

There are two basic contexts in which canonically irregular marriages can be dealt with in the internal forum. One is the case where there is ample reason to believe that despite appearances to the contrary, the first marriage was never truly a valid Christian marriage, though this cannot be proven by acceptable canonical procedures. In other words, it is a union that is not binding before God but cannot be demonstrated as such before the community. Traditionally, this situation poses an acceptable context for the approved practice of the I.F.S., according to the criteria outlined later in this chapter. A second and more complicated case involves a person or couple whose ostensibly valid, sacramental marriage has broken up and who have remarried, yet now seek to reestablish full communion with the Church. Such persons may sincerely hold that the new union is a true marriage for them, and may feel constrained to remain in the second marriage, for their own good and/or for the sake of their children. This case will be examined more carefully in our treatment of excommunication and access to the Eucharist in the next chapter.

Who may use the internal forum solution? The answer is not always immediately obvious, but there are many reasons why a formal declaration of nullity may be unobtainable. Key evidence may be lacking, or witnesses may be unwilling or unable to testify. The local tribunal may be non-functioning or may be so overwhelmed with caseloads that a delay of many months or even years can be expected, and the persons concerned may choose not to risk such a long delay in the desired second marriage. In light of the varying application of canonical jurisprudence, at times the only available tribunal may refuse to hear a case or may render a negative decision on grounds that are commonly accepted in other jurisdictions. While there is no dunning, some may balk at the prospect of having to pay hundreds of dollars to help defray the cost of the annulment process. Perhaps the parties concerned found the divorce so painful that they cannot reopen to outsiders the scarred-over wounds of past years, or they fear further rejection and more guilt if they submit to the annulment process. Other factors can make the formal annulment process unworkable, such as a concern for the welfare of the children of the former marriage if an estranged spouse is contacted, or fear that the former spouse or in-laws will react violently to such a move.

Again, some may sincerely believe that despite appearances, they never had a true marriage, though this may not be legally provable. Others may frankly concede that their first marriage was indeed valid and sacramental but was choked later on by the presence of sin. For these and many other reasons, the annulment process in the external forum may not be a workable means of resolving one's status in the eyes of the Church. It is then that the I.F.S. outlined below may be invoked.

Unfortunately, there are no uniform rules for applying the I.F.S. in light of traditional Catholic faith and practice, since the Holy See has not issued explicit norms and guidelines for its implementation. However, Rome has emphasized that couples using the internal forum solution may be reconciled to the Church and to the sacraments on two primary grounds. First, they must strive to live according to the norms of Christian moral principles. Second, they must also be willing to receive the sacraments in churches where their irregular status is unknown, should this be necessary to avoid scandal. Keeping these overriding principles in mind, let us list some more explicit guidelines for using the I.F.S.

The internal forum solution is a unique pastoral approach to the particularities of a given situation. It can only be used when it becomes clear that the possibilities of the external forum have been exhausted, that the spouses who have entered into a second marriage sincerely desire to participate in the sacramental life of the Church, have sought to avoid any scandal, are committed to maintaining a faithful, stable Christian union, have made amends and assumed responsibility for their part in the breakdown of the former marriage, and are providing for the education and support of the children of the present and previous marriages. There is no automatic, foolproof way of applying these guidelines to each particular situation; the process requires genuine spiritual discernment in both the couple and the pastoral minister. That spiritual discernment, however, is not easily attained; it requires a great deal of time, energy, and good will by all involved parties for the couple to arrive at a conscience decision based not on self-deceit or rationalization but on faith and on a sincere commitment to gospel values.

The pastoral minister, in addition to being warmly human and knowledgeable, can help the couple make a sincere and well-informed conscience decision by encouraging in them a reverence for the Church's teaching authority and for the ideal of the indissoluble Christian marriage. More specifically, the minister and the couple can discuss such questions as these:

1. Is the former marriage irreparably broken down, spiritually dead?
2. Are the couple living up to responsibilities owed to former spouses and to children by the prior marriages?
3. What is the couple's commitment to Christian life and values, and how are they willing to contribute to the local Christian community?
4. Are the responsibilities of the present marriage being authentically fulfilled?
5. In what measure are the couple willing to strive to avoid scandal and uphold the values of Christian marriage within the larger community?

If after sincere prayer and reflection on such questions the couple should decide to receive the sacraments, the pastoral minister should respect their conscience decision.

In a refreshingly clear letter issued to the priests of his diocese in October 1978, Bishop Bernard Gantner of the Diocese of Beaumont, Texas, offered much practical and sound pastoral advice on the application of the internal forum solution. Bishop Gantner emphasized that it is not a validation by a priest of a second marriage while the spouse from the first union is still alive, nor is it the granting of permission for a previously married person whose spouse is still alive to remarry in a Catholic Church ceremony. He stressed, too, that the internal forum solution is not a substitute for or a bypass of the annulment process but is a pastoral decision, made in the light of accepted moral-canonical practices applied to a remarried person, which allows him or her access to the sacraments of Penance and the Eucharist, if feasible. Under these conditions the remarried parties should express their willingness to validate the second marriage in the event of the death of the former spouse, and further, should agree to receive the sacraments only in a community where their irregular union is unknown if that is the only way to avoid giving scandal.

Bishop Gantner emphasized that the couple must be informed that this is a private accommodation based on their own informed consciences, reached in dialogue with a qualified pastoral minister. Furthermore, he stressed that they should recognize that the application of the I.F.S. in no way reflects a change in the traditional Catholic view that marriage is indissoluble. The couple's current marriage cannot be entered in the parish register, nor can any formal church certificate be issued, but this lack of official church approval need have no bearing upon the couple's access to the sacramental life of the Church.

Because the internal forum solution is a confidential, personal accommodation tailored to a couple's specific situation, it necessarily suffers from certain drawbacks. It is secret in nature, its application cannot be uniform, and both clergy and laity often misunderstand it. Moreover, by its very definition it cannot allow a public, official announcement that a given couple deserves its benefits. But despite these drawbacks it is a valuable pastoral tool that offers much healing and consolation to those in irregular canonical marriages who hunger for a deeper sense of union with God and with the Church. To fail to use its benefits for deserving couples is to miss an opportunity to exercise a genuine ministry of healing and reconciliation, and runs the risk of turning divorce and remarriage into an unforgivable sin.

The internal forum solution calls for a policy which cautiously and discriminatingly readmits to the sacraments those divorced and remarried Catholics who have conscientiously undertaken the process. The aim of its application is well expressed in the phrase of an ancient Christian writer, St. Gregory of Nazianzus: "Not to go too far in severity, not to shock by weak indulgence." The I.F.S. negotiates these twin shoals in order to arrive at a posture that respects Catholic doctrine and practice and is pastorally responsive.

Father John Finnegan, an active pastor and past president of the Canon Law Society of America, has captured as well as anyone the rationale for making use of the internal forum solution:

> If wisely communicated, this posture will not damage the Church's positive teaching on marriage permanence and fidelity. People are never scandalized by mercy and a desire to restore others to the sacraments and bring harmony and peace where once there had been alienation and discord. The "signs of the times" are calling for, crying out for, a Church of compassion, tenderness and healing. ("Marriage/Pastoral Care," *Origins* 5, August 28, 1975, p. 155)

The careful application of the internal forum solution is a prudent means of showing compassion and forgiveness to perhaps millions of divorced and remarried Catholics who cannot use the formal annulment process. It is a legitimate pastoral response, and one that people have a right to expect from the Church.

I PRAY FOR YOU . . . That does not mean that from time to time I pronounce certain words while thinking of you. It means that I feel responsible for you in my flesh and in my soul, that I carry you with me as a mother carries her child; that I wish to SHARE, I wish to draw entirely upon myself all the harm and all the suffering that menaces you and I offer to God all my darkness so that He may return it to you in LIGHT . . .

10

EXCOMMUNICATION AND ACCESS TO THE EUCHARIST

In one of the curious quirks of history, the American Catholic bishops, meeting in their Third Plenary Council at Baltimore in 1884 (the same session that gave rise to that famous document, *The Baltimore Catechism*), promulgated a new law that attached a penalty of automatic excommunication to any American Catholic who entered a second union after contracting a valid Catholic marriage. Strangely, this automatic incurral of excommunication applied only to American Catholics and was never a part of the universal discipline of the Roman Catholic Church, so that divorced and remarried Catholics were an anathema only in the continental United States (and, of course, its territories!). This gesture was seen by the bishops at the time as prudent means of holding together their largely immigrant flock. But in spite of its presumed good intentions, from the outset the law was experienced as a harsh, indiscriminate, and at times vindictive tool used to discipline those who had departed from the straight and narrow ways of the One True Church. It was experienced, too, as a countersign of the Church's healing and reconciling mission—a countersign that did little more than disenfranchise, alienate, and deeply wound many persons already suffering the pain of broken marriages.

In 1977 the National Conference of Catholic Bishops requested the pope to repeal the automatic ban of excommunication on American Catholics who contracted ecclesiastically invalid second marriages. (In doing this, they were finally reacting to the initiatives of a number of professional ministry groups and lay caucuses that culminated in the resolutions of the October, 1976, Call to Action conference held in Detroit that recommended a revision in the status of separated, divorced, and remarried persons in the Church.) Contrary to popular misconception, this ban had never applied to those Catholics who had simply divorced, but only to those who had *remarried* without the benefit of a church annulment while a former spouse from a valid marriage was still living. (Both the annulment process and the question of access to the Eucharist by remarried Catholics are treated in detail elsewhere in this book). Furthermore, the person's right to receive the sacraments was never affected by the fact of a divorce alone.

In outlining the rationale for this recent change in policy, Bishop Cletus O'Donnell of Madison, Wisconsin, himself an accomplished canonist and pastoral bishop, wrote:

> The positive dimensions of this action are very real. It welcomes back to the community of believers in Christ all who may have been separated by excommunication. It offers them a share in all of the public prayers of the church community. It restores their right to take part in church services. It removes certain canonical restrictions upon their participation in church life. It is a promise of help and support in the resolution of the burden of family life. Perhaps above all, it is a gesture of love and reconciliation from the other members of the church.

As a gesture of love and reconciliation, it served as a welcome first step for many who now knew that they could be hospitably received back into the fold and sent on their way in peace.

In our discussion of the internal forum solution in the previous chapter, it became evident that the annulment process may not offer a workable option for many divorced Catholics who are contemplating remarriage. For these persons, key questions often revolve around their access to the Eucharist. This problem should not be glossed over lightly, since as Paul emphasized in one of his letters, every Christian should be concerned with the worthy reception of the sacrament: " . . . whoever eats the bread or drinks the cup of the Lord unworthily sins against the body and blood of the Lord. A man should examine himself first; only then should he eat of the bread and drink of the cup" (1 Corinthians 11:27-28).

In some ways, this general principle spurred the American bishops at the Third Council of Baltimore in 1884 to issue the now-rescinded statute of automatic excommunication for divorced Catholics who remarried outside the Church, since the bishops felt that divorce and remarriage were grievous sins and threats to the faith of Catholics, an offense against both God and the Church. This position gained some strength with the promulgation of the *Code of Canon Law* in 1918, especially in two of its many provisions:

1. . . . those who in spite of the conjugal bond attempt another marriage, even a so-called civil marriage, are *ipso facto* infamous; and if, in spite of warning by the bishop, they persist in the illicit union, they are to be punished by excommunication or personal interdict, according to the gravity of the case. (Canon 2356)

2. They are to be excluded from the Eucharist who are publicly unworthy, such as those who are excommunicated, interdicted, and those who are manifestly infamous, unless their repentance and amendment is publicly known and they have previously repaired the public scandal they have caused. (Canon 855, no. 1)

One can perceive a certain strain of well-intentioned pragmatism in this approach. For instance, a local bishop might deny a public Mass of Christian Burial to a "manifestly infamous" underworld figure on the grounds that the sacrament could easily be abused and become a sham, a mockery. In this case, the concern of the Church is to protect the community of faith from public scandal or derision and to ensure that the sacrament has not become a perversion of what it is intended to be. In some ways, this same mentality undergirded the action of the American bishops at Baltimore in 1884 when they promulgated the automatic ban of excommunication for divorced Catholics who remarried. Such Catholics were totally cut off from the life of the Church for as long as their former spouse lived or as long as they persevered in their second union. To a certain extent, traces of this mentality can be detected in the Church's current official discipline about forbidding such persons access to the Eucharist, as we will see below. But to state the posture clearly, without an annulment a Catholic in a canonically irregular union may not receive the Eucharist. (Again, it is necessary to point out that this rule apples solely to divorced Catholics who have *remarried*; no special grounds have ever existed which automatically deprived divorced Catholics of access to any of the sacraments.)

This traditional Roman Catholic approach was reemphasized recently in a document on marriage doctrine published by the International Theological Commission, an elite consultative body to the Vatican's Congregation for the Doctrine of the Faith. In its "Propositions on the Doctrine of Christian Marriage" issued in 1978, the commission reiterated the standing discipline:

> The incompatibility of the state of remarried divorced persons with the precept and mystery of the paschal love of the Lord makes it impossible for these people to receive, in the Eucharist, the sign of unity with Christ. Access to eucharistic communion can only be had through penitence, which implies detestation of the sin committed and the firm purpose of not sinning again. (*Origins* 8, September 28, 1978, p. 239)

This same posture was repeated even more strongly by Pope John Paul II in his reflections based on the 1980 international Synod of Bishops and contained in his *Apostolic Exhortation on the Family*. In this document, the Holy Father noted that persons in canonically invalid marriages should be treated with great charity and welcomed into the life of their respective parish communities, but he noted that "the pastors of the Church will regrettably not be able to admit them to the sacraments" (no. 82). He spoke of the remarriage of divorced persons as "an evil . . . (that) must be faced with resolution and without delay," though he encouraged such persons not to consider themselves as separated from the Church, to attend Mass, pray, contribute to the life of the community, and raise their children in the faith. In an emphatic and unequivocal tone, the pope concluded (no. 84):

> . . . the church reaffirms her practice, which is based upon sacred scripture, of not admitting to eucharistic communion divorced persons who have remarried. They are unable to be admitted thereto from the fact that their state and condition of life objectively contradict that union of love between Christ and the Church which is signified and effected by the Eucharist. Besides this there is another special pastoral reason: If these people were admitted to the Eucharist the faithful would be led into error and confusion regarding the Church's teaching about the indissolubility of marriage.
>
> Reconciliation in the sacrament of penance, which would open the way to the Eucharist, can only be granted to those who, repenting of having broken the sign of the covenant and of fidelity to Christ, are sincerely ready to undertake a way of life that is no longer in contradiction to the indissolubility of marriage.
>
> This means, in practice, that when for serious reasons such as for example the children's upbringing, a man and a woman cannot satisfy the obligation to separate, they "take on themselves the duty to live in complete continence, that is, by abstinence from acts proper to married couples." (*Origins* 11, December 24, 1981, p. 465)

Each of these statements expresses the current official Roman Catholic teaching concerning remarried persons whose former spouses are still living but who have not received a decree of nullity. Before examining the rationale for this position, we must distinguish between the two main types of situations in which divorced and (non-canonically) remarried Catholics find themselves.

The first can be called the "conflict case." It exists when from its start a marriage lacked some essential element(s) needed for it to be considered valid and sacramental. Despite the fact that in appearance the couple contracted marriage in a Catholic religious ceremony, they know in their hearts that some impediment marked the marriage, though this may not be provable before a marriage tribunal. This type of case is resolvable according to the accepted moral-canonical principles outlined in the previous chapter in our treatment of the internal forum solution.

The second situation, known as the "hardship case," arises when a marriage deemed valid before God and the community breaks down, and one of the partners, now remarried, wishes to receive the sacraments of Reconciliation and Eucharist while remaining in the new union. This situation is far more difficult to resolve than the conflict situation, since the parties concerned concede that their now-defunct former marriages were once alive and truly sacramental. Initially, it seems there is no way to resolve such cases in the eyes of the Church. However, even here the stance of the Church is far more nuanced than a simple reading of its official teaching would imply, and a growing scholarly and pastoral consensus favors applying the I.F.S. to such cases. Many of the factors relevant to the conflict situation are operative here as well. Some reasons for applying the I.F.S. to hardship cases will be discussed below as we consider why some may choose to dissent respectfully from the posture spelled out by the pope and the International Theological Commission.

The primary objections raised against allowing non-canonically-remarried persons access to the Eucharist revolve around the following issues:

1. A determination not to approve a practice that objectively can be classified as leading to a state of sin.

2. A concern to avoid unwarranted scandal.

3. A desire to maintain unity in faith and discipline and to preserve the ideal of indissolubility in marriage.

4. A variety of understandings of the meaning of Church and of Eucharist.

Each of these four points will be considered in turn.

1. It is possible in some ways to speak of divorce and remarriage in the hardship case as constituting a state of sinfulness, since in virtually every instance some moral fault led to the erosion and eventual death of the relationship. Sin in the root sense of the word means to fall short of a goal, to miss the mark. Clearly, divorce among Christians does miss the mark of the intended ideal of marital permanence expressed by Jesus, and few would deny that they entered a sacramental marriage with the expectation that it would last forever. Regrettably, some marriages do die. But to apply the stigma of grave moral evil to every couple in the hardship situation and to assert that all of them are in a state of sin simply does not correspond to the experience of all couples or of their pastoral ministers.

Although some divorced and remarried persons may be in a state of serious sin, others may have sincerely repented their part in the failure of their first marriage, and may now be ready to commit themselves to a stable union, marked with mutual respect and love. Many deserving couples in the hardship case have hoped for acceptance in the eyes of the Church and have remained active, loyal Catholics. It is important to note that at times papal teaching and the practice of the Church have recognized that it is better for such couples to remain together, participate in Mass faithfully, and attend to the religious upbringing of their children. In other words, it is sometimes conceded that it may be desirable or even necessary for a couple to remain together, even in a canonically irregular union.

Every case must be considered on an individual basis, taking into account any mitigating circumstances. Even *The Baltimore Catechism* held that three conditions must be present before there is grave sin: (a) the act itself must be seriously wrong or considered so by the doer; (b) the person must be aware that the act is seriously wrong; (c) he or she must fully consent to it.

St. Paul pointedly reminds us that although sin abounds in the world, God's grace abounds more (Romans 5:20). For those who are sincerely repentant, no sin is beyond the scope of God's compassionate, healing power. Even recognizing the objectively sinful nature of divorce, to fail to provide for the spiritual needs of those who have divorced and remarried runs the risk of turning this practice into an unforgivable sin. God's mercy is stronger than human laws.

2. A deep justification exists for the Church's concern to guard against scandal in applying the internal forum solution. If a lax and widespread practice of admitting divorced and remarried persons to the sacraments were to develop, people might erroneously conclude that there is nothing wrong with remarrying after divorce, or that the Church is hedging on the ideal of marital permanence. Any such unchecked practice could disturb the faith of many clergy and laity alike, particularly of those who heroically have upheld the official church discipline, often at great personal cost.

For this reason, the response of Archbishop Jerome Hamer of the Vatican Congregation of the Doctrine of the Faith to the requests of the American bishops for clarification of the approved practice of the internal forum solution (in his letter of March 21, 1975) warrants special consideration. Archbishop Hamer noted that the application of the I.F.S. must be in the context of traditional moral theology, and pointed out that couples may be cautiously admitted to the sacraments on two conditions: (a) that they live according to the demands of Christian moral principles; (b) that they receive the sacraments in communities where scandal will be avoided.

As we have seen in our brief consideration of canon law affecting those who remarry outside the Church or those who attempt to receive Communion unworthily, the Church maintains a special concern that public scandal be avoided in the administration of the sacraments. But if the Christian community commits itself to preaching and supporting the gospel ideal of lifelong marital faithfulness and solidly commits its resources to achieving this goal, we need not fear taking a stance of Christ-like compassion toward well-disposed persons who have sought and found a genuine sense of peace and healing in a canonically irregular second marriage. As one American canonist, Father Thomas Green, points out:

In fact Catholic attitudes seem to be changing significantly on the issue, and a change in pastoral practice would probably not be a scandal but rather a source of encouragement and edification. Actually, the greater scandal may be the overly judgmental attitudes of certain individuals toward such divorcées and the failure of the institutional Church at times to provide the latter with adequate canonical and pastoral support in rebuilding their lives in Christ.

3. In addition to her firm determination not to countenance an objectively sinful practice and her concern to avoid scandal, a further compelling interest of the Church is to maintain unity of faith and discipline. The official teaching of the Church asserts that since divorcees have violated the Lord's call to marital permanence and have compromised her witness in this regard, they are unworthy to receive Communion. This official doctrine of the Church does present some difficulties, however.

In the flesh-and-blood reality of human lives, one must recognize that laws are not intended to bind in every possible circumstance and that, in the old Latin axiom, "The care of souls is the supreme law." Moral theology has long recognized this principle of reasonable exceptions as *epieikeia,* which Thomas Aquinas called "the crown of legal justice." Since some canonists have reliably estimated that about 40% of all divorced Catholics may have no *legally demonstrable* grounds for nullity, the urgent need for pastoral accommodation becomes all the more evident.

4. Our understanding of what is meant by Church and by Eucharist is crucially important in this question of who may or may not have access to the Eucharist. Experience has shown that separated or divorced Catholics who have remarried are not clamoring for recognition or for approval of "church divorce" and are often most ready to commit themselves to permanency and indissolubility in a second union, in contrast to the failure they experienced in their first marriage. They are primarily seeking deep, genuine acceptance from God and from the Christian community. This acceptance undoubtedly

finds its richest expression and its most powerful symbolization in the Eucharist. If we are inclined to understand the Eucharist today as the place where the members of the Christian community can gather and draw strength and nourishment at the table of the Lord in a meal of reconciliation, as contemporary Catholic theology envisions it, and if our understanding of what it means to belong to the Church has evolved as well, then the questions pertaining to the status of divorced and remarried Catholics and their access to the Eucharist can be seen in a different light.

The Church has recently come to the humble conclusion that it is, as the *Dogmatic Constitution on the Church* so ably expressed it, a "pilgrim people," constantly on the move, journeying to seek fulfillment of the values of the inbreaking Kingdom of God in the here and now, though painfully aware of the essential incompleteness of the present world, which, as the document states, "will attain her full perfection only in the glory of heaven" (no. 48). In the past, the Church spoke of itself as "a perfect society" and at times demonstrated a militancy and triumphalism that now have been largely laid to rest. The Church, like its members, is now more readily recognized as an "earthen vessel" through which God's grace can be communicated. If the predominant image of the Church is that of a company of believers striving to be holy yet still affected by the power of sin and evil, it is far easier for the Christian community to empathize and identify with those whose marriages have been choked through human sinfulness. For if, as Paul says, "sin abounds," the power of God's healing grace that abounds more must be shown in order to heal and uplift the brokenhearted.

In a formerly predominant piety, the Eucharist was sung of as *panis angelicus,* the bread of angels. But angels don't need it. The Eucharist was not created for disembodied spirits but for frail human beings who need spiritual nourishment and God's mercy. For hundreds of years it was the common practice to receive communion only once or twice a year, and to do so as a legal duty. Early in this century, though, Pope St. Pius X and then the *Code of Canon Law* both urged "frequent, even daily, communion" (Canon 81).

This renewal and development in the understanding of the Eucharist found its clearest articulation in the council documents of Vatican II. The *Constitution on the Sacred Liturgy* rightly perceived the Eucharist as the summit to which the Church's activity is directed and the source from which her power flows (no. 10). A similar understanding is contained in the *Dogmatic Constitution on the Church* (nos. 10-11) and the *Pastoral Constitution on the Church in the Modern World* (no. 38). The *Decree on the Ministry and Life of Priests* states unequivocally that "No Christian community can be built up unless it has its basis and center in the celebration of the most Holy Eucharist" (no. 6). It would seem obvious that if a marriage is to be understood as a "domestic church" and if its members are encouraged to strive to live out their Christian witness in the world, they must have access to the Eucharist. To require that spouses in a non-canonically-recognized marriage may receive Communion only if they maintain a "brother-sister relationship" (that is, without genital expression) is to deprive either of their natural rights in marriage or of the sacramental nourishment of the Eucharist—a means of "penance" that completely falsifies the meaning of both sacraments. An up-to-date understanding of the Eucharist is needed, so that the Church's pastoral practice can be responsibly carried out. The renewed emphasis in Catholic eucharistic theology stresses that receiving it is an integral part of faith and practice. The Eucharist has a twofold meaning, as a sign of unity and as a means of healing grace.

The theology behind the so-called "brother-sister arrangement" reflects an older Catholic religious understanding of marriage that viewed it as a contract for exchanging the rights and obligations suited for the procreation and education of children (Canon 1081). But this approach is narrow and excessively physiological. Today, marriage is seen as much more than a contract for sexual intercourse, which at times seemed to be the sum and substance of the older view. Formerly, those who engaged in intercourse in a second, canonically invalid marriage were seen as violating the rights of the ex-spouse, since he or she was viewed as still having a sole claim on the body of the former mate. Instead, today the paramount value seen in Christian marriage is the right to a communion of life and love, an intimate partnership where two persons give themselves totally to each other.

In light of the Catholic teaching about marriage that has evolved since Vatican II, one can conclude that the deprivation of sexual intimacy in a marriage is an equal violation of rights, and that the practice of the brother-sister arrangement has limited advisability. Serious and potentially harmful disorders can crop up for a couple and/or their children when the parents are denied sexual fulfillment in their marriage. Family harmony can be ruined and the couple decisively alienated from the teaching authority of the Church. Furthermore, the brother-sister arrangement runs counter to the positive stress on sexuality reflected in the *Pastoral Constitution on the Church in the Modern World,* which states: " . . . where the intimacy of married life is broken off, it is not rare for the faithfulness to be imperiled and its quality of fruitfulness ruined. For then the upbringing of the children and the courage to accept new ones are both endangered" (no. 51). This same common-sense approach is contained in the writings of St. Paul: "The husband should fulfill his conjugal obligations toward his wife, and the wife hers toward her husband. . . . Do not deprive one another, that Satan may not tempt you through your lack of self-control" (1 Corinthians 7:3,5).

Another accepted pastoral solution that attempts to accommodate those in the hardship situation is known as *dissimulation.* By definition, dissimulation is a knowing act by one in authority who pretends to ignore or overlook something unlawful in order to avoid a greater evil if disciplinary measures were invoked. As noted earlier in this chapter, Canon 2356 in the 1918 *Code of Canon Law* referred to divorced and remarried persons as bigamists and empowered the local bishop to excommunicate them and place them under personal interdict if they did not separate. Outside of the United States, this practice was restricted to severe cases only and was seldom invoked. Similarly, as we have seen, although Canon 855 turned away the publicly unworthy ("manifestly infamous") from receiving the Eucharist, in practice those whose irregular unions were unknown were frequently admitted and were supported in their desire to receive Communion, through the internal forum solution. The growth of a more responsive and open pastoral posture in the Catholic Church in recent years is evidenced in the assessment of a noted canonist, Father James Provost: "The general practice in the Church for more than the past decade has been to dissimulate even in regard to hardship situations, permitting the couple to remain together" ("Intolerable Marriage Situations Revisited," *The Jurist* 40:1, 1980, p. 143).

Although the many and delicate aspects of the formation of Catholic conscience receive extensive treatment in our chapter on family planning, it is necessary to point out here that some remarried persons may feel bound in conscience to refrain from receiving Communion. A primary pastoral consideration is attentiveness to where a couple's well-formed conscience is and what adherence to that means. Many people harm themselves when they do things that run counter to what they can later live with before others or before God. In spite of the renewed awareness and appreciation of active sacramental participation among Catholics, some may still conclude, within their own consciences, that they should not receive Communion. Such people should be assured that not all eucharistic graces are contained in receiving the consecrated elements of bread and wine, and that they can also experience the Real Presence of the Risen Lord within the celebration of the Mass, in the Scriptures, in the action and words of the priest, and in the presence of the assembled community (see the *Constitution on the Sacred Liturgy,* no. 7). The Catholic tradition speaks at times of "sacraments of desire" and of "spiritual Communion." Some may conscientiously conclude that this is the most suitable response for them, and such personal decisions should be respected and supported.

The most important conditioning factors for receiving the Eucharist worthily are a personal faith in the sacrament in harmony with the belief of the Church, and a proper disposition. It seems at best inconsistent that a lifelong Catholic whose first marriage has ended should be deprived of access to the Eucharist, while at the same time the Church now urges the extension of eucharistic hospitality to separated brethren, when such a gesture "provides a sharing in the means of grace" and "the gaining of needed grace sometimes commends it" (*Decree on Ecumenism,* no. 8). A divorced and remarried Eastern Orthodox Christian who has received a church blessing for a second marriage may be extended eucharistic hospitality in a Roman Catholic liturgical setting from time to time. Why not extend the same sign of reconciliation and healing to the millions of sincere divorced Roman Catholics who have remarried? All the reader need do is substitute the adjective "remarried" for "Eastern" in the following passage from Vatican II's *Decree on the Eastern Churches* (no. 26) to draw an appropriate parallel:

> Divine Law forbids any common worship which would damage the unity of the Church, or involve formal acceptance of falsehood or the danger of deviation in the faith, of scandal, or of indifferentism. At the same time, pastoral experience clearly shows that with respect to our Eastern brethren there should and can be taken into consideration various circumstances affecting individuals, wherein the unity of the Church is not jeopardized nor are intolerable risks involved, but in which salvation itself and the spiritual profit of souls are urgently at issue.
>
> Hence, in view of special circumstances of time, place, and personage, the Catholic Church has often adopted and now adopts a milder policy, offering to all the means of salvation and an example of charity among Christians through participation in the sacraments. . . .

On these grounds, prudent admission to the Eucharist should be strongly contemplated and encouraged for (non-canonically) remarried Catholics for whom the application of the annulment process is not possible, providing that such toleration does not call into question the essential indissolubility of marriage and that the first marriage is demonstrated to be irretrievably broken. If serious moral fault led to the death of the first marriage, that fault must be recognized and repented, and the spouses of the new union should demonstrate a sincere desire for the nourishment offered at the table of the Lord, a desire that stems from their own hearts and consciences. The couple and the pastoral person with whom they enter into spiritual direction must take care that no justified scandal is stirred up in the local community because of this practice, and in particular must be careful not to foster the misimpression that such a pastoral accommodation represents a faltering on the Church's total witness to the ideal of the indissolubility of Christian marriage.

Ultimately, the questions pertaining to the internal forum solution can be resolved only over the course of time and through dialogue and spiritual discernment. But in the final analysis, Catholicism holds that the decision to receive or not to receive Communion rests in the heart of the individual. The role of the priest or pastoral minister is to preside over a spiritual direction process by which the couple reflect on the situation, pray, and finally come to a decision under the guidance of the Holy Spirit as to whether it is appropriate for them to take Communion. No priest or bishop or even the pope can make this decision for a person. Nor are there any ready means for streamlining the process. A remarried couple, or a couple about to enter a non-canonically-recognized second marriage, should be prepared to invest a significant amount of time and energy to resolve these sensitive matters, while striving to remain open to the working of the Holy Spirit and to seek the best possible response.

Part Three

PREPARING FOR
REMARRIAGE

11

PROSPECTS FOR A SUCCESSFUL MARRIAGE TODAY

Marriage in America today is so riddled with pain, confusion, and heartbreak that some observers have called it the country's number one disaster area. Current research has shown that only about 10% of all married couples claim to feel really happy and fulfilled. Another 20% or so say that they are happy some of the time, while the remaining 70% range from being bored and noncommittal, to hanging on for the sake of the children, to deserting the spouse and children, to terminating the marriage legally by seeking a divorce. The United States now boasts the dubious distinction of having the highest divorce rate in the world. If we take into account not only divorce but the situation in which the spouses separate and move to different households with no intention of reuniting, one can guess that well over half the marriages presently being formed will at one time sustain a significant break.

While in 1980 the number of marriages peaked in America, 32% of those unions entered into were remarriages. It is estimated that 75% of the women and 83% of the men whose marriages end in divorce will eventually remarry. This trend toward remarriage increases slightly each year and is a barometer of the basic shift occurring within the institution of marriage: Marital separation and divorce are becoming more of a transitional state than a permanent life-style among Americans. The fact that so many marriages have been tried and found wanting does not necessarily indicate that people have given up hope in marriage. On the contrary, the high remarriage rate indicates that people have far from abandoned such hope. Marriage is still a means by which most persons establish their place in society, and it serves as a primary determiner of self. It offers people a sense of who they are, of what to feel and do, and of how to act toward others. Marriage provides many people with both their primary reason for being and their code of conduct by which to live. The fact that marriage has eroded so much in our present culture makes it no less important today than it ever was. In fact, if we bear in mind the near universality with which people enter into marriage in the United States, we can readily assume that most Americans find marriage crucial to their well-being and personal fulfillment.

While it is true that the divorce rate in the United States doubled from the mid 1960s through the late 1970s (for some of the reasons to be discussed below), the tapering off of that trend by the early 1980s belies a deeper hunger for intimacy and rootedness that so often eludes the victims of marital breakdown. Some 95% of all Americans will one day marry, and of those who divorce, roughly 80% will remarry. In spite of the more tentative approach that some have adopted toward marriage, most Americans still view marriage as the best means of living out the sometimes conflicting goals that society has set before them. The human and pastoral dimensions of the problems of separation, divorce, and remarriage have been increasingly recognized within the Christian community, as one can see in the comment of Bishop Cletus O'Donnell: "There's hardly any family among us that hasn't been touched by divorce. It is one of the foremost problems facing the Church today."

From a social perspective, it is interesting to note that half the divorces registered in the U.S. happen within the first seven years of marriage. While the highest rate shows up in the second year, when "the honeymoon is over," fewer than 10% of all divorces take place during that year. More than a third of all divorces happen after ten years of marriage, and one out of ten fails after twenty years or more, often as a casualty of the "empty-nest syndrome." Statistically, the older persons are when they divorce, the longer it takes for them to remarry and the less likely it is that they will actually do so.

There are many reasons for so much marital disruption and failure in American society today. Poverty and financial strain are still among the primary causes of marital breakdown. A marriage can bend or break because of the strong socioeconomic tugs and pressures exerted upon it, such as the growing numbers of working wives and the increased financial and emotional independence that women have achieved apart from the household in recent decades. This shift, triggered by economic change, has applied pressure to many marriages. In addition, legal barriers to divorce have given way in many respects because more women can afford legal fees or avail themselves of free legal aid, and because "no-fault" divorce laws have appeared in many states. In short, the advances of feminism and changes in the work force have applied additional pressure to marital situations. Today it can simply no longer be concluded that if a husband's job falls prey to the I.B.M. (I've Been Moved) syndrome, his wife will concur readily and forget her own personal and professional commitments. Because of all these overlapping factors, many marriages are experiencing levels of strain today that were unknown in past generations.

The relatively new phenomenon of the extended life expectancy of married couples today is also a highly complicating factor. At present, a beginning couple may reasonably expect to live together for almost fifty years, which means struggling through many stages of their lives together.

The inroads of secular culture have made their mark as well. Many have come to accept the ready accessibility of divorce, especially since most major social and religious taboos and stigmas have waned. Ironically, some have replaced an excessively romantic view of marriage with an equally romantic view of divorce, mistakenly embracing divorce as a cure-all for their problems. In the past, as in the case of a chronically alcoholic spouse, many Catholics would have resigned themselves to the situation of an intolerable marriage, accepting it as a cross to bear, with relief coming only through the death of one of the partners. However, today a greater sense of freedom and independence prevails. This, coupled with recent changes in canonical and pastoral practice (discussed in our treatment of the annulment process and the internal forum solution), has offered many the opportunity to end a seemingly intolerable situation. Believing that they will not jeopardize their faith commitment or be treated like pariahs should they seek divorce, many in fact have begun to feel for the first time that they have a right to a certain measure of personal happiness and fulfillment that their first union failed to provide.

Another major cause of marital failure in the United States today is service-connected disabilities stemming from the Vietnam conflict. It is estimated that one out of every five of the servicemen who were stationed overseas during the Indo-China war are clinically disabled emotionally in ways that can make them "walking time bombs" in a marital relationship. The highly publicized incidents of heavily armed veterans who have taken over banks or churches may be symbolic eruptions of the same emotional conflicts that have plagued the marriages of so many of these "walking wounded."

To sum up in Bob Dylan's line, "You don't need a weatherman to know which way the wind blows." Clearly, living out a sacramental marriage as the Church envisions and gives witness to it has become increasingly difficult. But individuals and couples caught up in marital crises can still find ways of resolving them. Besides studying this book, especially the sections on marriage enrichment and conflict resolution, they can, for instance, pledge themselves to do everything within their power to foster real communication with their intended spouse. They can seek outside help, when necessary. And they can determine to invest the time and effort and pain needed to make their marriage work and grow in spite of the many roadblocks facing it today.

12

DATING AGAIN

For a person craving companionship and struggling to regain a single identity, a new relationship can do much to reduce the level of pain and frustration, boost the sense of self-esteem, and reestablish the feeling of being lovable and worthwhile again. Every person has a need for intimacy, for sharing in a deep bond with another where the risks and pain experienced can be outweighed by the benefits of closeness, security, and mutual trust. This kind of intimate bonding requires not only mutual openness but also the reciprocal, respectful protection of each other's uniqueness.

As two persons begin to invest in a new relationship, they must put aside their fears and become vulnerable again by revealing hidden aspects of themselves to each other. To avoid repeating unattractive or self-defeating traits that may have marked past relationships, the couple should strive to become aware of such traits and be willing to change or discard them. They need to see that new patterns of communicating and relating are available and have to be learned. Some adjustments and give-and-take are always in order. But if the couple are determined to make the new relationship last, in time they can build up trust that will enable them to weather the everyday tugs and pulls of life together.

As we have noted elsewhere in this book, 80% of all persons whose marriages end in divorce eventually remarry. The average widow's age is 54, and 75% of all presently married women can expect to be widowed. In terms of percentages, there is little significant difference between young divorced persons and widowed persons who eventually remarry (though the older one becomes, the less likely one is to remarry, and men are more likely to remarry than women). The very fact that so many persons remarry, however, does not assure one that selecting a new mate will be easy. If one bears in mind that more second marriages than first marriages end in divorce, this should serve to awaken one to some of the complications involved in dating again and in selecting a new mate.

Many unresolved feelings remain to be sorted out after the end of a marriage. Typically, people start dating again because they need and want to belong to and to develop strong bonds of intimacy with someone. At the same time, though, they fear becoming involved in another dead-end relationship that will end just the way the preceding one did—they will be rejected and then go through the same dreadful experience of loss.

Dating again involves other problems. For instance, it is a well-known fact that often formerly married persons unconsciously gravitate toward another person who will provide the same neurotic gratifications that marked their first marriage. Although such persons frequently believe that their new relationship will be totally different from the old one, they may be unaware that the new person has the same behavioral traits as the old one, and so the same unhealthy patterns of interaction will be perpetuated.

Moreover, people tend to involve themselves in relationships "on the rebound." Loneliness may prompt them to seek out another with whom they can mourn the passing of the now-lost relationship. It is important to recognize that it takes time to recover emotionally and to build a new life: usually from two to four years. Keeping this important time frame in mind from the beginning makes it less likely that a person will become involved with another person too soon and will thereby short-circuit the time needed to relate freely and healthily to another.

A middle-aged person who begins to date again often feels awkward. Often, he or she may feel totally inadequate and out of place, thinking, "This is crazy. I haven't had a date since I was engaged, and now here I am, expected to act like a teenager again." Because the experience can be so new and different, a number of cautions are in order. First, the person should be aware that despite the very real and threatening level of anxiety present, learning to love again presents great opportunities if one allows the relationship sufficient time and energy to develop and unfold at its own pace, without a lot of externally applied pressures. One must avoid trying to relive or re-create the past and instead must view the new relationship on its own merits, without imposing a lot of preconceived notions on the other person or on the future of the relationship.

The way a person views himself or herself invariably shapes the process of recovery and the ability to relate to another in an intimate, mutually sustaining fashion. If significant areas of conflict or tension arise, they should be checked out and worked through, with respect for the differences and the uniqueness of each person involved. One must always maintain a balance between being sensitive to the needs of the other and asserting one's own perceived needs. Often, checking things out with trusted friends or family members or with a competent professional can help to clarify one's perceptions of the possibilities of the new relationship. The measure of approval and affirmation that such persons express is often a good barometer for gauging how successful one might be in that relationship.

Establishing mutuality of trust and interests is often a vital indicator of whether a friendship will flourish. This insight is well articulated by the noted British author C.S. Lewis in his book *The Four Loves* (New York: Harcourt Brace Jovanovich, 1960, pp. 96-97):

> Friendship arises out of mere companionship when two or more of the companions discover that they have in common some insight or interest or even taste which the others do not share and which, till that moment, each believed to be his own unique treasure (or burden). . . .two persons discover one another when, whether

with immense difficulties and semi-articulate fumblings or with what would seem to us amazing and elliptical speed, they share this vision—it is then that friendship is born. And instantly they stand together in an immense solitude.

Ultimately, sharing in friendship is exactly that: sharing a vision, insight, or interest. For that reason, one of the best ways of coming to know another person on a deep level is to find a way in which both persons can give expression to such vision, or insight, or interest, as in special-interest groups, adult education classes, evening or weekend college courses, church groups for widowed or divorced persons, human potential groups, sports leagues, or theater guilds.

Contrary to popular myth, there is nothing to support the claim that opposites attract and help make a marriage hold together. If one is seeking a permanent, inner commitment that encourages a highly loving, emotionally intimate, and sexually free gift of selves, one will almost always find it in a marriage marked by similar social, economic, and educational background, occupational status, age, emotional stability, ability to express and receive warmth and to reinforce one's own and the other's sense of self-esteem, as well as similar needs for independence and assertiveness and a mutually acceptable circle of family and friends. If many of these factors are weak or lacking in the new relationship, the odds of its taking hold and lasting are not great.

The consuming passion for an attachment figure may impel many to enter into fleeting and superficial liaisons, as we will see in our treatment of sexuality. Playing the bar scene or singles clubs or seeking cheap intimacy in other ways should be recognized for what it is: a dead-end pattern of relating. What such persons are really seeking is true friendship, which is seldom found in such settings. There is a great deal of enduring wisdom in the words of the Roman orator Cicero: "What is a friend but a partner in love, to whom you unite and attach your soul, and with whom you blend so as to move from being two to becoming one, to whom you can entrust yourself as to a second self?" For that kind of friendship to develop, essential elements are time, openness to change, a willingness to disclose aspects of oneself, and the ability to listen and to communicate clearly and openly while remaining in touch with one's own feelings.

One of the most solid bits of advice that can be offered to a person beginning to date again is: Take things slowly and deliberately, and seek to establish mutual interests, trust, and love in a setting where it is unlikely that you will view the other person solely as a sexual object or as a source of immediate satisfaction of your own needs but for his or her own uniqueness and personhood. The social, educational, and religious interest groups mentioned a few paragraphs back often supply such a desirable setting.

As we have noted, a person whose marriage has recently ended is very vulnerable and needs to be careful about not getting into deeper pain than he or she already feels. From the emotional perspective, if the person resolutely determines to reforge his or her own way, work through the phases of loneliness, and begin the recovery process while supported by others, while recognizing the two-to-four-year normal time that such a process takes, then there is a far greater likelihood of success in the new relationship. In the meantime, family, friends, clubs, and social or religious groups can serve as a mainstay of emotional support while the reality of the new relationship is sorted through and tested out. It is only over the course of time that a realistic judgment can be made on whether the new relationship is "marriage material."

The final major consideration to be borne in mind with dating concerns the reactions of the children, which we will consider in some detail in our treatment of the new extended family. Some say this factor is the number one culprit in remarriage. The children's response to the dating of a custodial parent in particular can be a cause of great concern to all involved persons, especially if it is marked by petty jealousies and rivalries. Frequently a son will be angry and resentful when his mother is more accessible and emotionally closer to a number of male companions than to him. In such a situation, a child may become hostile and antagonistic to both the parent and the date, and may try to sabotage the relationship by stirring up trouble between them, sulking or throwing temper tantrums, faking sickness, nose-diving academically, fighting with peers or siblings, or engaging in drug abuse, illicit sex, or vandalism. All these patterns of acting out are screens for the child's attempt to keep the parent from "abandoning" him or her. If the child is acting particularly obnoxiously towards the date, he or she may be convinced that such behavior will persuade the mother to drop the relationship. Along this line, it is important that the children be exposed only to those dates who have established a sustaining, meaningful relationship with the natural parent. As the noted child psychiatrist Richard Gardner states, "In this way, the parent avoids exposing the children to the seemingly endless parade—the situation most likely to produce difficulties for the children."

One of the most positive values that a new "surrogate parent" figure can offer to the children is a presence that can help to make up for the absent parent. And if the custodial parent is clear, open, and direct in sharing with the children, his or her own increased happiness and fulfillment will in all likelihood be transmitted to them and will both deepen their own sense of security and well-being and make the parent seem more acceptable. Then they may in the course of time perceive the new arrangement as less threatening and, in fact, quite palatable. The custodial parent who appears happy and fulfilled and is now operating on a more even emotional base can very probably show the proper amount of love and affection to the children. If this is the case, they will likely come to recognize and appreciate this and will be far better able to accept the new parent figure.

A final word of caution is in order concerning the tendency of some custodial parents to seek out and secure a prospective spouse "for the sake of the children," so that there will be a mother or father figure once again adorning the household. While it is undeniably true that children's needs should be carefully taken into account in such a decision, the highest priority ought to be given to the needs of the adults involved, not of the children. In the same way that competent counselors discourage couples in intolerable marriages from staying together for the sake of the children, so too single parents ought to refrain from marrying solely or primarily on account of the children's welfare. While it is usually undeniable from the psychological perspective that children fare better in a household where both mother and father figures are present, what really matters is the *quality* of the relationship. At times the presence of a certain parent can be more of a detriment than an asset.

The children's reaction to a new dating arrangement is always a complicated affair. This interplay needs to be treated delicately, and where necessary a counselor may help iron out the wrinkles for all concerned. As we will see in discussing the new extended family, the way family and close friends accept the new union can be the most important single determiner of its future success. So a good question for the newly dating, previously married person is, to borrow the phrase of New York's Ed Koch, "How'm I doing?" If one is willing to pose this question to loved ones and take their replies seriously, then one should have a fairly clear reading of where things stand—a valuable addition to one's own intuition about the prospects of the relationship.

13

DEALING WITH SEXUALITY

Only within the past generation or so has the Catholic community begun to formulate a more positive approach to human sexuality. It has shifted from the former ends-oriented approach of seeing marital sexuality strictly in terms of the procreation and education of children and has taken a more positive, personalistic tack. Often, the spouses' attitudes toward their sexuality have been colored by the former overly negative views toward sexual expression, even in marriage. But today we have come to a more comfortable realization of the positive role that genital sexual expression plays in marriage; we see human sexuality in its right context as a gift of the Creator God. An active and fulfilling sex life, based on the right attitude toward sexuality and maintained at a mature level, is an indispensable means for a couple to achieve their full human potential in the marriage relationship. It will make for happiness and growth in intimacy for a couple not only in the transition period following their remarriage but throughout their marriage, even into old age.

The normal point of departure for a Christian understanding of human sexuality may seem a bit confusing, since Jesus himself said next to nothing on the matter that is preserved in the New Testament, and Paul's views were heavily colored by his own single life-style and his pressing conviction that since the end-times were imminent, Christians would do better to "make converts, not love." The approach to sexuality that the early followers of Jesus took was further tainted by the pagan philosophy of Stoicism, which held that sexual intercourse was always tinged with some sort of evil and that only its pro-creative purpose could make it morally tolerable. This negative mindset regarding sexuality was reinforced in the Church by the enormous influence of St. Augustine, who though a religious genius and a champion of Catholic orthodoxy, always retained a jaded view of sexuality, perhaps as the residue of his own unhappy early affairs or of the matter-denying heresies of his youth. It was Augustine's view that Original Sin was transmitted through the act of sexual intercourse and that, by extension, sexual acts were always colored by sinfulness.

The key insight of contemporary Catholic sexual morality is that genital sexual expression so deeply involves aspects of the human person that only the stable and enduring union known as marriage provides the context where human love can be offered most generously and authentically, in a setting secure enough to foster and sustain new life. Such a sexual union creates a depth of bonding between the spouses and fosters the upbringing of children so that the family unit can be drawn together and experience a warm, open, mutual exchange of love.

Human sexuality is a dimension of the person that moves him or her toward completion, fulfillment, and wholeness. While the ideal of Christian sexuality in marriage might never be realized in its entirety, it stands as a constant goal for spouses to strive for while seeking closeness with each other and with God. This kind of authentic sexual expression presumes and requires an initial grounding in a trusting, caring, loving relationship that leads to commitment to and responsibility for the other. It is painfully obvious that at times sexual expression can be selfish, manipulative, exploitative, or even violent—a means of inflicting harm upon the self or another. But it can serve as a catalyst for growth and maturity, a visible means of representing God's presence and the power of his love acting in human hearts and lives. This pivotal insight into Christian married love was well articulated by Pope John Paul II in one of his weekly audiences (see *L'Osservatore Romano,* January 7, 1980, p. 2):

Man becomes the "image and likeness" of God not only through his humanity, but also through the communion of persons which man and woman form right from the beginning. . . . Humankind becomes the image of God not so much in the moment of solitude as in the moment of communion. . . . Right from the beginning there is not only an image in which there is reflected the solitude of a person who rules the world, but also, and essentially, an image of an inscrutable divine communication of persons. . . .

In the moment of communion in marital intercourse, a man and a woman can experience in ecstatic union their own mutuality as well as a sacramentalization of the presence of God in their midst.

In marriage, sexual expression is a most sacred good that can serve to deepen and enhance the union of life and love that binds the couple together. However, the couple should take care to see that their sexual conduct is wholesome and upright, conducive to growth in the relationship. It should be honest, responsible, faithful, joyful, self- and other-enriching, and life-serving in order to be love in the image of God.

Although it is clear that sex can serve an enormously positive function in a marriage relationship, obviously it can also be distorted or abused. Sexual expression can be used as a means of futilely trying to re-create or make up for one's past. It can be a way of expressing anger toward an ex-spouse while feeling alone or abandoned, or a means of acting out self-hatred while seeing oneself as a failure or worthless. Or it can be a vain attempt to reinforce one's sense of masculinity or femininity. The desire of a hurting person to fulfill various levels of human need, such as physical touch and stroking, emotional support, a sense of security in a relationship, or the validation of self-worth can lead to shallow sexual liaisons and end in disaster.

Some of these dangers may befall persons who are separated or divorced, widows or widowers. Since they have already lived out their sexuality in a relationship with one person, they now have to struggle in a new way to redefine their sexual selves and carve out a new single identity. Such a radical new social and emotional posture can leave a widowed or divorced person reeling with a sense of being overwhelmed, confused, vulnerable, and overloaded with a host of powerful and at times conflicting sexual impulses and feelings.

For some divorced persons, certain lingering feelings of attachment may prompt further sexual involvement with the former spouse, even though both may consider the relationship irreparably broken. Though a source of some gratification, this kind of union is generally short-lived. Other divorced or widowed persons may find themselves engaging in short-term encounters with a succession of other partners, in a flagging attempt to reaffirm their diminished sense of personal worth and attractiveness. Others may seek out a longer-term relationship with one extramarital partner. Ultimately, however, these patterns of relating are usually self-defeating and destructive, and leave the divorced or widowed person vulnerable to exploitation as he or she seeks attachment to another and strives to satisfy a wide range of unfulfilled needs.

Often, men respond to the end of their marriage with a diminished sense of self-worth and frequently vent their anger upon women and make them victims of their unresolved hostility. If such men are reasonably attractive and cagy, they may assume the role of a wolf engaged in a seemingly insatiable sexual hunt that diminishes in intensity only if and when their need for personal assurance is satisfied. While they may eventually recover emotionally, they may never come to realize why they were so incessantly driven to pursue such sexual conquests, and they may in retrospect even boast of this phase of their lives. On account of the pitfalls accompanying this type of unsatisfying behavior, divorce-adjustment counselors often advise their clients on purely psychological grounds, to refrain from any genital sexual contact for at least a year after the end of their marriage.

When their marriage has eroded, many women and men go through phases of having brief affairs, though women seem instinctively less driven by a wish to bolster their sagging self-esteem than by a compelling desire for an attachment figure. This desire may at times be coupled with a conscious or unconscious will to act out unresolved anger toward the former spouse, self, or God because of feeling lost or abandoned. The sad paradox is that while in these instances sex is sought as an antidote for pain and loneliness, it often serves only to build in distance and emerges as shallow, tentative, and boring, a travesty of its intended meaning and little more than a form of exploitation. Such indiscriminate sexual liaisons may appear to be a remedy for pain and loneliness, but sooner or later their true value is revealed, and the pain and loneliness that have been masked are only compounded by so much sex and so little meaning or joy in any of it.

From an objective standpoint the reasons behind this kind of acting out can sometimes be readily discerned. Perhaps some act that way because of boredom, curiosity, or sexual frustration. Or it may be a "get-even" gesture or a veiled signal for recognition. For some it may be a symptomatic eruption of hostility or a means of reasserting one's sexual identity while experiencing a midlife "passage." For others it may betray an immature personality or a lack of ego strength.

The bottom line is that apart from the context of marriage, sexual intimacy that is quickly sought or easily given can short-circuit the possibility of achieving true and lasting intimacy. To live out Christian ideals may be a constant struggle in which we fall short, miss the mark, and stand in need of healing and forgiveness. But the previously married person is well advised to be wary of the pitfalls of sexual intimacy prior to having truly come to know and love the other in a committed way; such intimacy can readily stifle the development of the relationship and, to use the phrase of Faulkner, lapse into the "same frantic steeplechase after nothing."

The immediate satisfaction of the "pleasure principle" ought not to be mistaken for true growth in love; relationships that are quickly fixed on the sexual plane may be doomed to remain there. Sadly, when a couple are locked into this pattern of relating they often remain strangers to each other and never disclose the measure of self needed to sustain a committed relationship. What on the surface seems to be love may in fact be fleeting or illusory. In such relationships, very often either or both persons are being used, and ultimately someone or some ones get burned.

14

MAKING A PERMANENT COMMITMENT: ASSESSING NEEDS AND MATCHING PERSONALITIES

In marriage, two people give of themselves and strive to satisfy their mutual needs as they continue to grow together in love. What distinguishes marriage from other human relationships, though, is the intensity of the sharing, for in marriage two persons experience a degree of bonding unmatched in human relationships. As they pledge their lives to each other forever, they know they will experience good times and bad, pleasure and pain, conflict and healing. This range of feelings and experiences is all a part of the "two-in-one fleshness" that constitutes marriage. But if a marriage is to survive and grow, certain conditioning factors must be taken into account. Not every couple are capable of the total mutual gift of persons that marriage calls for. If the chemistry between two spouses is not right, then their differences will be heightened by virtue of the intensity of the marriage bond, and conflict and unfulfillment are bound to take hold.

What qualities seem to be common to happy, successful marriages? Emotional maturity, mental stability, financial responsibility, and the ability to deal with the ordinary strains and stresses that arise in everyday life are essential features. So is the ability to be affirming, to express personal warmth, and to be sexually compatible. And if a couple's educational background, income level, and religious and political orientations are similar, the likelihood of a workable, lasting marriage is enhanced. Research has shown that if spouses have similar social backgrounds and bring compatible values, interests, goals, and expectations to the relationship, they are less likely to experience marital strife.

As a couple prepare to remarry, they should explore personal issues and the expectations that each has of the other and of the relationship. Questions concerning communication styles, gender roles, money matters, leisure-time activities, sexual needs, relationships with family and friends, child-rearing, religion, and politics can loom as prime areas of difficulty and dissatisfaction. The couple need to check all these things thoroughly so that they can fully come to know and appreciate the aspects of themselves and of the other that will affect their life together and can determine their compatibility and "marriage-ability."

As mentioned earlier, it takes time to recover from a marriage that has ended. Experts say that one can usually be ready for a new commitment in the third or fourth year following the end of a previous marriage. Normal, well-adjusted persons need that much time to recover emotionally; anyone who feels the need to remarry in the first or second year should carefully question whether the real driving force behind that need is the desire to be taken care of rather than the wish to grow mutually with another. If the second marriage is to succeed, the one who has been previously married needs to bring to it the strength of having survived the loss of the former marriage; one must not expect the new spouse to fill every conceivable need. As a couple grow in intimacy based on vulnerability, warmth, and caring love, their relationship will be marked with growing mutual trust and respect, and they can be optimistic about the prospects for a happy new marriage. But they should be very wary of making a hasty commitment, of acting "on the rebound."

First, the couple need to identify old ways of relating that marked the former marriage. They need to know that those old ways of relating are not the only ones available. If they want to form an intimate relationship that is more gratifying than the previous ones, they must be willing to recognize, acknowledge, work through, and shed old habits and patterns that hindered previous relationships. Otherwise they run the risk of repeating the destructive patterns of the former relationships: The faces and the names of the spouses will have changed, but the same old patterns of relating will be reproduced.

A common example of this is the person who remarries an active alcoholic after having suffered through the ups and downs of an alcoholic household in the previous marriage. Because the alcoholic spouse generally fills an unspoken need for the non-alcoholic one, he or she is often drawn to repeat the same unhealthy patterns of relating that led to the break-up of the previous marriage. Even though the person entering the new union may firmly believe that this marriage will be different, he or she may fail to recognize that the prospective spouse carries the same psychological baggage as the former one, and the same unhealthy patterns of interaction are bound to resurface.

So the couple should seek to determine what went wrong in a previous marriage of either spouse and should openly share their own stories and experiences with each other. Neurotic patterns of behavior can carry over into new relationships. They can "hook" something in the other party and draw the couple together in the first place but can ultimately destroy the relationship by hindering the possibilities for full participation and growth in a mutually enriching marriage. On account of this, the couple should seek to know themselves and each other well before making a permanent commitment. The growing complexity of married life in our culture makes it difficult enough for a couple to make it together today. More than ever before, greater attention to psychological and social factors is needed in the process of premarital preparation.

If the couple cannot come to some clear measure of insight about the potential areas of difficulty in their relationship, they should seek out a competent counselor to assist in the process of premarital evaluation. Certain tools have been developed for facilitating this task, in particular the Premarital Inventory (P.M.I.) developed by Bess Associates, the Myers-Briggs personality inventory, and PREPARE, developed by the Family Social Science Center of the University of Minnesota by Dr. David Olson. Any such resource is only an aid to helping the couple gauge their readiness for marriage; it is never a failsafe predictor for measuring whether there will be problems in the relationship. But they are useful tools, if wisely used and interpreted by someone with counseling expertise. If the couple opt to take the P.M.I., PREPARE, or a comparable diagnostic test, they should also sit down with a competent counselor to obtain a reading of the results and to apply it to themselves and to their prospects for making it in a new marriage.

In sum, each person entering a marriage has unique strengths and weaknesses, hang-ups and virtues, good and bad habits. If the couple are remarrying out of their mutual strength, the odds are that they will succeed in marriage. If they are marrying out of weakness (from financial pressure, for the sake of the children, or out of some neurotic need), then serious and potentially disastrous difficulties are bound to follow. If a couple planning marriage search out potential problem areas within themselves and in each other and frankly acknowledge and discuss them, particularly with the guidance of an experienced helping professional, the likelihood of recognizing and working through areas of potential difficulty is good. In short, a couple preparing for remarriage should very carefully assess needs and match personalities before making the total commitment of persons that Christian marriage calls for.

15

INTERFAITH MARRIAGES

The last third of the twentieth century has rightly been dubbed the beginning of the "ecumenical age," and nowhere are the benefits and difficulties of interfaith sharing so readily apparent as in interreligious, or "mixed," marriages. At the start of the eighties, fully 40% of Catholic marriages celebrated in the United States were ecumenical, and this figure takes into account only those marriages entered into under Catholic Church auspices or with the proper church dispensation. Some observers claim that if one were to take into account the total number of marriages in the general population involving Catholics and non-Catholics who marry without official church authorization, perhaps as many as 60% of all marriages involving baptized Roman Catholics are interreligious. Obviously, the growing frequency of such marriages gives rise to a number of questions and concerns.

First, regardless of the religious affiliation of the partners, if the marriage is to succeed there should be substantial agreement on and acceptance of the values and ideals of Christian marriage that are spelled out in the ritual. Statistically, it has been shown that couples with no religious affiliation have the highest divorce rate, while the next highest grouping are those in interfaith marriages. A shared religious heritage can be the glue that holds a marriage together "in good times and in bad, in sickness and in health," and it offers many advantages to a couple contemplating marriage. However, a great deal of strength and complementarity can be derived from an interreligious marriage, especially in light of the fact that today fewer and fewer spouses are moved to convert to the faith of the other in order to bridge religious gaps, a practice that was relatively common several decades ago. In this ecumenical era, the formerly discouraged practice of a Catholic and non-Catholic marrying has now become increasingly routine, though there are still a number of significant differences that a couple should examine and resolve before they enter into the commitments of marriage.

Some key points of conflict often are questions of shared prayer and worship and the religious upbringing of the children. Well in advance of the anticipated wedding date, the couple should seriously enter into dialogue about how their differing religious convictions might affect their married life. If they cannot come to an essential agreement about faith matters without compromising their consciences, they might well decide to delay their marriage, since such indecision could give rise to great conflict and tension later on. The experience of many couples, however, is that an earnest attempt to understand each other's faith commitment and to explore existing differences will ordinarily allow for a greater honesty and flow of mutual love. If the couple strive sincerely to know and appreciate each other's religious heritage, they can deeply enrich each other's life. They should stress the commonality and points of intersection of their respective faiths and agree to respect the differences. One of the most important cautions is for them to resolve not to lapse into religious indifference or apathy. All the important decisions concerning faith and practice should be made in advance of the wedding itself, and if a mutually acceptable resolution is struck, the odds are good that the couple will find some common ground where they can pray and unite themselves more closely with each other and with God, and develop a richer married life.

This idea was clealy voiced by Cardinal Willebrands when he spoke to the Synod of World Bishops on the topic of family life ministry in the fall of 1980:

It can be said of the marriages of two Christians who have been baptized in different churches, as it is of a marriage between two Catholics, that their union is a true sacrament and gives rise to a "domestic church"; that the partners are called to a unity which reflects the unity of Christ with the Church; that the family, as a family, is bound to bear witness before the world, a witness based on that spiritual union which is founded on a common faith and hope, and works through love. . . .

Rather than being a sign of contradiction, the marriage of two Christians of different religious backgrounds can promote deeper union if the couple are able to view their marriage in light of the covenant union of Christ and the Church. In fact, the Vatican II *Decree on Ecumenism* specified that the "spirituality of married life" is an area where there are great prospects for "ecumenical progress."

Some of the most difficult questions posed by mixed marriages revolve around the religious upbringing of the children. The world view of a child can certainly be enhanced by an exposure to the religious traditions of both his or her parents, though a clear choice should be presented to avert unnecessary conflict or confusion, both for the child's good and to maintain the peace of the family. Since 1971, the American Catholic bishops have required only the Roman Catholic party to make a promise, either orally or in writing, that he or she will remain faithful to the Catholic tradition and will seek to raise any children born of the new marriage as Catholics, "while respecting the religious convictions of the non-Catholic partner, and without placing their conjugal life in jeopardy." The formula states: "I reaffirm my faith in Jesus Christ, and with God's help intend to continue living that faith in the Catholic Church. I promise to do all in my power to share the faith I received with our children by having them baptized and reared as Catholics." The non-Catholic party is not required to make the promise, though he or she must be clearly advised of its intent and ramifications for the Catholic spouse.

The key issue involved in the promise centers around the intention of the Roman Catholic party to do "all within my power" to have the children baptized and raised as Catholics. This pledge should be understood as an obligation of the Catholic party to make a sincere and dedicated effort to raise and educate the children in the Catholic faith. It should not be understood as an ironclad mandate that must be maintained at all costs, should it result in "placing their conjugal life in jeopardy" by causing deep quarreling and resentment that would choke the marriage or harm the emotional or spiritual well-being of the children. In any event, the children should always be given a balanced appreciation of the traditions and beliefs of both their parents. It is the task of the priest or pastoral minister, in the premarital preparation process, to file a petition for a mixed-marriage dispensation with the local diocesan chancery, asking the bishop to waive the impediment of mixed religion, a permission that today is rather routinely granted.

At times, the couple may ask the local bishop for permission to have a non-Catholic wedding ceremony, in particular if one of the parties is actively associated with another faith community or desires to have the wedding celebrated within his or her own church. This permission may be secured in order to achieve family harmony and avoid unnecessary alienation, or to acknowledge a special relationship that the couple might have with a non-Catholic clergyperson. Ordinarily the presence of a Catholic priest or deacon should be sought in order to satisfy the "canonical form" required for validity (the form requires the presence of the Church's minister, and at least two witnesses), though at times the local bishop may waive this requirement for a pastoral reason. In any event, only one clergy member should serve as the presiding minister, to elicit the exchange of vows, witness the mutual consent of the bride and groom, and call upon God to bless the marriage. If a Catholic priest or deacon is invited to share in an ecumenical service in another house of worship, he might best concern himself with reading a Scripture passage or preaching the wedding sermon, by agreement with the presiding minister. Should an ecumenical marriage take place at a Catholic church, the visiting minister, if any, would function by doing one of the readings or, with special delegation, by preaching the sermon.

For the reasons outlined in the chapter on planning the ceremony, it is better for interfaith marriages to take place outside the context of a nuptial Mass, so that all those present may participate fully in the ceremony. Insofar as is practical, the religious dimensions of both faith traditions should be brought out within the marriage rite.

16

MARRYING OUTSIDE
THE CHURCH

As we have seen in considering interfaith marriages, 40% of the weddings witnessed under Roman Catholic auspices in the United States today are "mixed marriages" involving baptized Catholics and persons of a different religious tradition. We have also seen that if one were to include the number of baptized Catholics who marry without proper church dispensation, either civilly or in another religious ceremony, this figure might climb to as high as 60%. In other words, in the total picture, possibly six out of every ten baptized Catholics in the United States will marry a non-Catholic. Many will do so in a civil or religious ceremony apart from Catholic auspices, or "outside the Church." Since this is an increasing phenomenon, it would seem appropriate to examine the distinctions between church marriage and civil marriage and to survey the kinds of marriages involving Catholics that take place apart from the Catholic marriage rite, both with and without proper church authorization.

First, it is important to dwell on the most basic distinction between church marriage and civil marriage. Civil marriage is a social contract that establishes a conjugal union. But the church sees marriage as a sacrament in which husband and wife consecrate themselves to each other and to the world in such a way that the love of Christ is expressed in their union of life and love in a freely chosen, exclusive, permanently intended bond that is open to the gift of children. Except in extraordinary cases, civil marriage is never viewed as being real marriage for baptized Catholics, unless the local bishop has granted a dispensation from the usual form for a valid pastoral reason or unless a qualified church witness (a priest or deacon) is unavailable for a long time. In such circumstances, the civil ceremony itself can serve as an extraordinary canonical form for the reception of the sacrament, providing that the spouses intend their marriage in the way the Church understands and expresses it.

Theologians like St. Thomas Aquinas have long held that the essence of Christian marriage rests not only in the sacramental nature of the relationship but on the human values it signifies as well, such as friendship, mutual caring, and self-giving love. These latter are virtues that might be found in any person of good will, and are the mark of successful secular as well as sacramental marriages. At present we are witnessing a more open attitude in the Church toward civil marriage and its human, life-affirming values, though sacramental marriage under church auspices is still regarded as a vital, public sign of faith and of lived Christian witness in the world. While Roman Catholics and Eastern Orthodox both require validly recognized sacramental marriages of their own members to be witnessed in the canonical form (that is, before a priest or deacon and two witnesses and according to a recognized ritual including Scripture readings, the exchange of consent of the couple, and nuptial blessings), today the positive values of civil marriage are being more readily recognized by theologians and laity alike. This is reflected in the report of the pope's hand-picked International Theological Commission on "Propositions on the Doctrine of Christian Marriage" issued in 1978, which states in part: "For non-Christians and even for non-Catholic Christians, this civil ceremony can have constitutive value both as legitimate marriage and as sacramental marriage." There is a growing recognition that marriage outside the auspices of the Catholic Church can indeed have a lasting, redeeming import for those entering into it, though this may be a "less perfect" response than an explicitly sacramental marriage, especially when the marriage involves a baptized Catholic. Part of this shift in emphasis is reflected in the repeal of the automatic ban of excommunication for any American Catholic who married outside of the canonical form without proper church authorization, which remained on the books until 1966. Today, no such discipline exists.

Many marriages involving Catholics and non-Catholics do take place within the canonical form of the Catholic church ceremony, though at times they may be witnessed in a non-Catholic liturgical setting as well. For instance, an interreligious couple might wish to be married in a Protestant church ceremony in order to maintain peace and harmony in the family, or because the non-Catholic party has a close tie with a particular house of worship. Even when such marriages are performed in a non-Catholic setting, it is increasingly common to obtain from the diocesan chancery a dispensation from the impediment of mixed religion and from the canonical form. And while ordinarily the presence of a Catholic priest or deacon is required to satisfy the canonical form, the local bishop may waive this too for a legitimate pastoral reason.

A slightly more complicated situation might arise when a Catholic and a Jew marry. Since some Jews find it difficult to attend a religious service in a Christian church, a local bishop may allow the ceremony to take place in a synagogue, in an inter-faith chapel on a college campus, at the home of the bride or groom, or, as the last resort, in a catering establishment. Here again this accommodation is made for pastoral reasons and out of respect for the sensitivities of the persons involved.

There are many reasons why a couple may choose to enter into a marriage without proper church authorization. It is possible that one of the parties' prior marriages ended in divorce or separation. Now, the Catholic tradition holds that marriages witnessed sacramentally and physically consummated are indissoluble by any individual on his or her own authority and end only with the death of one of the spouses; so if no clear grounds for a declaration of marriage nullity exist (see our treatment of the annulment process), the original marriage is technically viewed by the Church as a source of binding marital rights and obligations, regardless of whether or not the marriage has irremediably ended. While both of the persons in the second marriage may feel free *in conscience* to undertake the new union, as long as a spouse from the first marriage still lives it is impossible for the Catholic Church formally to recognize the second marriage as a valid, sacramental union. In such cases, the prudent application of the possibilities outlined in our treatment of the internal forum solution remains to be explored, and the extensive guidelines presented there would direct the response of Catholics desiring to maintain their status in good faith with their church.

While Roman Catholic theology holds that for the marriage of a baptized Catholic (or Orthodox) to be valid and sacramental it must be witnessed in the canonical form and consummated physically, paradoxically it can consider the religious (or even *civil*) marriage of a non-Catholic to be sacramental, provided that the essential intentionality of the couple for a permanent, exclusive, freely entered union open to children is present. Since the desire to enter a second marriage may reveal a situation in which the non-Catholic party has been previously married and divorced, it is quite possible that the non-Catholic party may balk at the prospect of having to submit to the annulment process conducted by a Catholic marriage tribunal, though he or she never lived under that discipline and perhaps never intended the first union to be the kind of marriage envisioned by the Catholic Church.

In practice, there are very many instances in which divorced Protestants or Jews who married in a religious or civil ceremony are required to submit to the annulment process before the Catholic Church will declare them free to marry in the canonical form. This can cause much consternation for non-Catholics, who often place relatively little value on church law or canonical structures. Yet in some diocesan tribunals, as many as 70% of all annulments are granted for marriages entered into by two *non-Catholics*! If the non-Catholic party does not, in conscience, appear willing to submit to the annulment process, then the internal forum solution may be the only option available to the Catholic party once he or she has remarried, to reconcile his or her church status.

Another possibility may involve a Catholic who in conscience feels unable to enter into the annulment process because he or she is convinced that the original marriage was indeed once valid but was later choked by sin; or a Catholic who for psychological reasons is advised not to begin the annulment process; or a Catholic who simply lacks the evidence needed to prepare a suitable petition. Under such circumstances, the couple would then have to marry in either a civil or a non-Catholic religious ceremony. They should carefully consider the criteria posed in the chapters on the annulment process and the internal forum solution prior to reaching any decision, and should seek out competent pastoral counsel before taking any big steps.

The internal forum solution is a pastoral compromise on an individual basis that departs from the official Catholic posture, as recently repeated by Pope John Paul II in "The Apostolic Exhortation on the Family," in which the Holy Father stated:

> Reconciliation in the sacrament of penance, which would open the way to the eucharist, can only be granted to those who, repenting of having broken the sign of the covenant and of fidelity to Christ, are sincerely ready to undertake a way of life that is no longer in contradiction to the indissolubility of marriage.
>
> This means, in practice, that when for serious reasons such as for example the children's upbringing, a man and a woman cannot satisfy the obligation to separate, they "take on themselves the obligation to live in complete continence, that is, by abstinence from the acts proper to married couples." (*Origins,* Dec. 24, 1981, p. 465)

While the pope reiterated the traditional Catholic doctrine that a husband and wife in a non-canonically-recognized marriage must live "as brother and sister" in order to have access to Penance and the Eucharist, many responsible pastors would point out that the crowning jewel of moral theology is the recognition that the couple's informed consciences can prevail in individual circumstances, if they have entered a process of authentic spiritual direction with a qualified pastoral guide, feel that they must remain together for their own good and for the good of any children that are part of the union, and sincerely believe that they need the fuller sacramental nourishment that current church discipline does not allow for. This posture is explored fully in our treatment of access to the Eucharist, as well as in the chapter on the internal forum solution.

Today there are other circumstances in which a non-Catholic (or even a baptized Catholic) may wish to marry a Catholic but does not subscribe to the sacramental understanding of marriage as the Church articulates it, as a freely entered, exclusive, permanent bond open to the gift of children. If one of the parties were adamantly opposed to such values, by virtue of that fact he or she could not enter into the marriage covenant as the Church intends it. The Church would view such a marriage as invalid from the start. If the prospective spouses cannot agree on such key areas, however, they would be well advised to consider postponing or scrapping their wedding plans altogether until they can see eye to eye.

We have already seen that only about 2% of all divorced Catholics in the United States have received annulments. So it is easy to assume that the great majority of the rest who remarry (and more than 80% of those whose marriages end in divorce, for instance, do remarry sooner or later) will eventually do so "outside the Church." While this may be a painful fact of life reflecting current Catholic Church discipline, it does not and should not necessarily signal the end of one's link with the Catholic Church community. Unless and until some unforeseen sweeping changes are made in the Catholic Church's doctrine and practice on marriage (perhaps along the lines of retrieving the "principle of economy" that existed in the West until the High Middle Ages), millions of Catholics in second marriage situations will be forced to marry outside their own communion. This may be a less perfect response in an unfinished world, but for those to whom the annulment process does not seem to offer a real alternative it may be best to marry civilly or in another religious tradition, in accord with what some would call the theology of compromise.

17

PLANNING THE CEREMONY

Ironically, one of the facets of marriage preparation that often receives the least attention is planning the wedding ceremony, which frequently yields precedence to matters of dress, the invitation list, or the reception dinner. Yet if the ceremony is truly to reflect the wishes, tastes, and needs of the couple, they must engage actively in planning and developing it.

If the ceremony is to carry true meaning it should emphasize the significance of the promises being made and the motives from which they spring. The marriage of two Christians is both a joyful and a solemn occasion, so the wedding liturgy should emphasize both the happiness and the seriousness with which the couple are entering into this new commitment. As a rule of thumb, any element that reflects either gushy sentimentality or grim sobriety should be avoided.

By nature, most second marriage ceremonies tend to be smaller and more intimate than the first time around, though in the celebration the couple should not ignore the fact of a previous marriage. Undeniably, there are many differences in going through a second wedding, particularly if one or both of the intended spouses have children from a prior marriage. There are many delicate considerations that should go into planning a tasteful and tactful remarriage ceremony (some of which are beyond the scope of this chapter, since its primary focus is on the religious aspects of the wedding ceremony).

Anyone contemplating remarriage would do well to read an excellent little book entitled *The New Etiquette Guide to Getting*

Married Again, by Marjabelle Young Stewart (Avon Books, 1981), a clear, concise, comprehensive treatment of many practical concerns, such as invitations and the guest list, expenses, children, dress, and the reception. For the religious dimensions of the wedding celebration, the best available resources are Jeremy Harrington, OFM, *Your Wedding: Planning Your Own Ceremony* (St. Anthony Messenger Press, 1974), Father Christopher Aridas, *Your Catholic Wedding* (Doubleday Image, 1982), and Father Joseph Champlin, *Together for Life* (Ave Maria Press, 1979 revision), all of which are available in inexpensive paperback editions.

Anyone who was married before the 1970 revision of the ritual might notice that a number of elements found in the former rite are missing today. The old wedding ritual primarily emphasized that two families were being joined by a contract, and it implied a distinct inequality between the man and the woman in that it asked her but not him to "love, honor, *and obey*." The present ritual reflects a more positive and relational view of Christian marriage and more clearly portrays marriage as the free and joyful offering of love between two equal persons.

Two major options are to be considered regarding the ceremony: It may take place either within or outside the context of the Mass. In both cases it has the same essential elements. It is usually more appropriate for the marriage of a Catholic and non-Catholic to take place outside of Mass, because the various churches differ in their teachings and sacramental life and because the non-Catholics present may find the Mass unfamiliar and discomforting and may not be able to participate fully.

The couple themselves are the primary ministers of the sacrament, but it is also witnessed on behalf of the whole Christian community by the celebrant, the maid (or matron) of honor and best man, and all who have gathered for the liturgy. The celebrant greets the couple and their families and friends in a cordial way and invites them to listen to and reflect on the scriptural readings that form the Liturgy of the Word. It is highly recommended that from the options posed in the ritual the couple choose scriptural passages that are most personally meaningful to themselves and that express their love for each other. A member of the wedding party or relative or close friend of the couple is welcome to do one or more of the readings, though this person should be comfortable with the idea of reading publicly and should thoroughly practice the reading. The marriage rite provides for a reading from the Old Testament, a responsorial Psalm (preferably sung), a selection from one of the New Testament letters, and a Gospel passage— the latter to be read by the celebrant prior to preaching the homily. Non-biblical readings do not lend themselves well to the Liturgy of the Word. If desired, an appropriate reading could be inserted as a meditation piece later in the ceremony.

The heart of the meaning of Christian marriage is reflected in the brief exchange of questions and answers that follows the homily and in the declaration of consent of bride and groom. The celebrant asks the couple to state before God and the Church that they are free to marry, that they will be totally faithful to each other until death, and they will be open to children (if the latter remains a possibility). As they respond affirmatively, they join their right hands to declare their consent to this new union. The rings are then exchanged, and after the prayers of intercession a final nuptial blessing closes the ceremony.

One of the most important aspects of the wedding ceremony is the choice of music. It is the responsibility of the celebrant and of the parish musician, along with the couple, to judge the authentically artistic and liturgically appropriate quality of the music proposed. The lyrics of the songs should echo the values of the Gospel and express the faith of the Church. Often, popular music is better suited for the reception hall than for the church service. The twofold criteria of aesthetic quality and liturgical propriety should always be observed in selecting music for a wedding. Does the music desired communicate something about Christian marriage as a free, mutual, permanent exchange of self-giving love? When it is sung or heard will it enhance the ceremony, or will it detract from it? Is it tasteful, or merely trendy? Musical selections may be used as the processional, recessional, and meditation pieces, as a response to the first reading, and in a nuptial Mass, for the ordinary sung parts of the liturgy.

Most church musicians are happy to make a selection of wedding music available to couples preparing for marriage, and many public libraries stock books that give appropriate musical settings. If something other than organ music is desired, the organist or parish music director can often suggest another musician, such as a guitarist, who would be able to play at the wedding, though his or her fee may be higher than that of the usual church musician. In some parishes the regular organist's fee must be paid even if another musician's services are retained, in order to offer the church musician some measure of financial security. The best advice is: Check well in advance with the celebrant and church musician on the local policies concerning music.

If flowers are desired, arrangements can be made through a local florist. It is good to instruct photographers to maintain a discreet and low-profile presence. Care should be taken to see that the ceremony begins on time, as there may be another service scheduled soon after the wedding. The celebrant should have the marriage license in hand before the wedding day, and prior to the ceremony the best man should see to it that the ring or rings are readily available. Some couples may choose to include a special candle-lighting ceremony within the liturgy; if so, this should be discussed with the celebrant in advance.

The couple may wish to compose their own wedding prayer or *credo*. This is preferable to writing their own *vows*, since personally composed vows tend to overlay these commitments with flowery prose, and at times they serve only to obscure rather than enhance the meaning of the ceremony. By their nature the vows must reflect the couple's freely-made commitment to permanence, fidelity, and openness to children that are the essential elements of sacramental marriage. In any event, the American Catholic bishops addressed this point in the newsletter of the Bishops' Committee on the Liturgy (August/September, 1981) by reemphasizing that only approved formulas found in the marriage ritual may be used in the celebration:

> A couple is not free to compose their own declaration of consent. While the couple may well find language of their own to express very profoundly their consent and covenant which they undertake, this is a central, ritual, and ecclesial act, and they have a responsibility to the community of believers assembled, that is, the church before which they manifest their consent, to use language clearly and certainly conformable to the church's faith and understanding of the sacrament.

In light of this directive, a wedding prayer or *credo* could be prepared in writing and inserted later into the ceremony, or within the nuptial Mass as part of the prayer of the faithful or as a post-communion meditation, where it would more fittingly express the sentiments of the couple and still respect the integrity of the liturgy.

If the marriage involves persons of two different faith traditions, the participation of a minister or rabbi is usually welcomed. This can be arranged well in advance so that his or her part in the ceremony can be smoothly facilitated. Following the completion of the marriage-preparation requirements, a follow-up meeting takes place with the celebrant so that the couple can finalize plans before the wedding rehearsal. Every wedding can and should be an occasion of great joy. But as with most things in life, there is usually a direct relationship between the amount of time and energy the couple have invested in the planning process and the benefits they reap. If the couple take a caring, active, and personal interest in preparing the ceremony along with the celebrant, they can be assured that it will reflect their tastes and needs and will remain for many years as a happy and spiritually nourishing memory.

Part Four

ADJUSTING TO A
NEW LIFE-STYLE

18

RELATING TO THE
NEW EXTENDED FAMILY

To paraphrase Abraham Lincoln, "The Lord must have loved step-parents—he made so many of them!" In the United States today, more than twenty-five million husbands and wives in second marriages are step-parents. More than fifteen million children live in these households. Each passing year, more than half a million men and women and their children are added to these ranks. Even should the present trend level off somewhat, step-families—produced when a parent remarries after separation, divorce, or the death of a spouse—have emerged as an increasingly common facet of the American social landscape. As we have already seen, 80% of those whose marriages end eventually remarry. The younger the persons involved, the greater the likelihood of their remarriage.

While most couples entering a second marriage maintain lofty fantasies about the way their new situation will work out, these visions are often soon dashed by the many problems that inherently plague such families. This is especially true when children are involved, since the new parental figure who enters their lives often becomes the target for their displaced hostility (they may already be feeling guilty, abandoned, lost, or rejected because they have lost a natural parent). The step-parent often becomes a lightning rod for the children's churned-up feelings, a sort of scapegoat on whom the children can vent their anger.

Step-parents must realistically face the fact that the deck is stacked against them from the outset and must acknowledge how difficult it will be to forge a healthy, loving relationship with their future stepchildren. It isn't too difficult to see that the overwhelmingly negative stereotypes of the wicked stepmother or stepfather, so familiar from the fairy tales contained in children's books, still supply the dominant images by which most people view step-parents, especially stepmothers. Even when the natural parent may have callously abandoned his or her children, the step-parent, as a replacement figure, may still bear the brunt of the children's unfocused anger. It is hard to face up to this and not to take it too personally. But a step-parent with insight into the situation will likely be able to accept and grow fond of the children in the course of time. Eventually, the children may also come to appreciate and accept the step-parent and enter into a warm, meaningful, caring relationship.

Some experts feel that the most crucial factor affecting the future happiness of a remarriage involving stepchildren is the extent to which the children come to accept the new parent. And if a second marriage has the approval and support not only of the spouse's children but of family and friends as well, then it has more possibility of growing and flourishing, in spite of the difficult period of readjustment marking the life of a new, extended family. But if the couple have significant reservations about how their children will react in the new family setting, they are well advised to seek out premarital counseling on how to ease the adjustment. All too many people naively shrug before the fact and say, "It'll work out." More often than not, it doesn't. A couple facing such a potentially disastrous situation must be willing to invest time and energy in developing a healthy relationship with the children. An experienced, competent counselor can be immensely helpful in showing them how to do that.

It is important to realize from the very beginning that the children of a new union will typically show a high level of "negative" feelings towards both the natural parent and the future step-parent when confronted with the new living arrangement: especially anger, guilt, resentment, and fear. If the adults can recognize and help to work through the children's feelings in a non-threatening way, then these moments of conflict can serve as a springboard for growth in the relationship. Again, consulting an experienced helping professional can be most valuable in seeking to resolve the tension.

Because the new spouse introduces another potent force into the family structure, the natural parent can reasonably expect a change in feelings from his or her children. Both one's own children and one's new stepchildren are bound to experience a flood of confused and mixed feelings. It is important that the children of the intended union hear early on of the impending marriage, and not learn of it second hand from relatives or friends. While it is not wise to seek the children's "permission" for marrying the new spouse, children should be told that a serious relationship is developing and be allowed to know the prospective step-parent gradually, over the course of time. The future step-parent would benefit from spending time with the other person's children, so that he or she can get to know them and appreciate them as individuals. One should keep in mind that it takes a fair amount of time for a child to adjust to a new member in the family, and should plan accordingly. But if the prospective step-parent treats each child as an individual and makes a sincere effort to get to know each one, the transition to a new family life will almost certainly happen more smoothly.

Perhaps the best advice that can be offered to prospective step-parents is to take things slowly and allow time for new relationships to develop naturally. At times, a step-parent's sense of insecurity and need to feel wanted may prompt him or her to try to "win the children over" by a sort of bribery— for instance, by lavishing affection, praise, or gifts. Actually, this kind of approach is more likely to turn the children off and may retard or possibly destroy altogether the prospects for cultivating a healthy relationship.

The natural parent is well-advised to take time to sit down with the children and share with them the feelings he or she has for their prospective step-parent. Aware of the bonding that existed and often still exists between the children and the now-absent natural parent, it might also be good to offer them some tangible reminder of that person, like a special photograph or other memento. In this way the children will feel more reassured that their non-custodial parent is not being squeezed out of their lives and that in some way the absent parent will always remain as mother or father to them.

A word is in order on the potential difficulties facing households with adolescent children. The insertion of a new figure (the step-parent) into the family structure can trigger a round of shockwaves of sexual and competitive jealousies. Teenagers often misread the love and affection shown to the step-parent as a withdrawal of love and affection from themselves or other siblings. This often causes a high level of anxiety mixed with anger. Under these circumstances the adolescent will frequently "act out" in order to get attention: He or she may resist discipline, become disruptive at school or in the community, nose-dive scholastically, engage in acts of vandalism, experiment with alcohol, drugs, and sex, and seek to build in excessive distance in relationships by withdrawing farther from the natural parent and step-parent. At times, the sexual arousal, competitive rivalries, frustration, anger, and guilt that the teenaged stepchild experiences in regard to the opposite-sexed step-parent can become so destructive that the only solution may be for the family to get intensive family therapy or for the child to move out of the household for a while for a cooling-off period. Such situations should be defused early on. By recognizing the climate that breeds resentment and feeds on relational strife and by seeking to head it off, the couple can do much to provide for their own peace of mind and that of the whole family. To be sure, the teen years are a time of much ambivalence and growing pains, and one can always expect some rough sledding in the family situation. But if the difficulties encountered seem to be out of control, outside help may be necessary.

Living in an extended family is a complicated affair. The couple contemplating remarriage would do well to read up on this area and to talk extensively with other people who have been through the experience. A key to the whole adjustment process consists in understanding the level of the relationship and the responsibilities that the other spouse feels toward his or her children, and in respecting and getting to know each child as an individual.

It is important for the couple to stand firm in maintaining a set of household rules and responsibilities and in delegating tasks to the children. If the couple agree to present a "united front" to the children, they will probably not fall prey to the "divide-and-conquer" strategy sometimes used so effectively by children as they play parents one against the other. Above all, the most valuable tool in the adjustment process is a good sense of humor and a willingness to be patient and forgiving when things go wrong.

Adjusting to life in a new household takes time, effort, and a certain amount of "blood, sweat, and tears." But the situation can be handled more productively if all parties involved come to the realization that they must almost certainly pass through a number of stages as they struggle to come to terms with their new reality. Divorce adjustment counselor Mel Krantzler, in *Learning to Love Again,* outlines four such phases. First, he says, the step-parent must realize that he or she is an outsider who will be mistrusted by the children as coming into a new family and perhaps taking away their remaining natural parent's love for them. Second, the step-parent may come to be accepted by the children as a tolerable acquaintance but may still be kept at arm's length (perhaps because of the unconscious fear that he or she may eventually leave them, as the real parent now being replaced once did). Third, over the course of time a genuine measure of trust and acceptance can develop. Finally, the step-parent may possibly become a loved and cherished friend; but, as Krantzler points out, he or she will never really become a loved *parent*.

Since the step-parent can never fully take the place of the absent natural parent in the minds of most children, the step-parent ought to be called by a name different from that of his or her predecessor. For instance, if the children called their father "Daddy," it might be easier for them to adjust to a replacement figure by calling him "Pop," "Father," or by his first name or nickname, if this should seem appropriate. Since the expectations and the realities of the new relationship are often so totally different from what preceded it, it is easier for the children to sort out their feelings for the now-absent parent and the newly introduced figure if they are able to call the latter by another name.

Conflicts and tension often develop in second-marriage situations because of unmet (and unrealistic) expectations on everyone's part. If the natural parent and the step-parent are clear on the unfolding possibilities of their new marriage and family life, and if they take into account the needs and limitations of the children affected by the new union, they will have a far better chance of establishing a happy and stable household.

19

ESTABLISHING A
NEW HOUSEHOLD

A basic problem for the single parent is living in a household where there is no other adult—no adult with whom to talk or express one's own feelings and ideas, no adult to share the responsibility of running the household. Remarriage often solves many of these difficulties, but it also creates a set of new ones so complicated and so crucial that they can be the acid test of the couple's relationship. The overall difficulty is: How do we merge two households and establish a new one?

The questions raised are so complex and so important that both partners must be determined to compromise and bend as much as possible. Also, they should try to work out all the major decisions (for instance, the ownership of property) and agree upon a resolution before they enter the new marriage, insofar as that is possible.

One major problem is deciding where to live. For at least one of the partners—perhaps both—the marriage will mean pulling up stakes and moving to a new place. That is always an emotionally unsettling experience, but once it is completed, many other matters fall into place. In some instances, it might be advisable for both of the spouses to leave their present living arrangements and start out anew in another place. This of course may not be practical when taking into consideration the children and questions of easy access to job, shopping, and recreational sites, to say nothing of the matter of personal preference and life-style and the expense involved in moving, renting, or home financing.

Once the couple have decided where to live, they must next agree on whether to rent or buy the new dwelling, which can either be a private home, apartment, condominium, or co-op. As a rule of thumb, it can take from six months to a year to scout out an acceptable place and take care of the preparatory details, let alone accomplish the actual move. Some times of the year are inherently better suited than others for moving. For instance, summer allows the spouses to use vacation time to get settled in; and if there are children involved, they can more easily change schools and make new friends at the park, beach, or pool.

Apart from all the personal and interpersonal and financial adjustments that have been touched on elsewhere in this book, setting up a new household carries with it many practical problems. A primary concern revolves around outfitting the new home. It is already hard enough to determine what to do with two sets of furniture, troves of personal mementos, and assorted household goods and furnishings. The couple should be ready to bend and compromise as much as possible, particularly on the matter of what objects to keep and what to discard. Insofar as possible, it is wise for all such questions to be worked out and agreed upon prior to entering into the new marriage. As the couple discuss and settle upon what is needed to outfit their home, they should sort through what each of them already possesses and be willing to discard any items that do not have a functional or sentimental value. In all likelihood, some new items will be needed (and perhaps these can be the object of a second marriage "shower"), such as place settings, flatware, glasses, linens, or living-room and bedroom funiture. Naturally, the couple may choose to retain much of what each has already possessed from prior living arrangements, but a new "common stock" may help them feel more invested in their new living situation and can serve to stave off or eliminate some of the possessiveness and potential conflict that can mar second marriages.

A further area of concern is the division of household labor. As the new spouses begin to settle into married life and redefine their roles and responsibilities, they should know that the reality of their new situation is reflected and tested most clearly in how they approach the sharing of household chores. This is a delicate area that requires negotiation in advance, with the couple aware that there will always be a need for some give-and-take. It is important that the couple know each other's likes and dislikes and be willing to compromise. The man, for instance, may love to cook but may loathe doing pots and dishes. The woman may be an avid cleaner but may hate ironing or doing windows. One may be mechanically inclined, the other all thumbs. Some trade-offs are always in order, and perhaps the best solution is to work out a rotation schedule whereby each member of the household (including the children) alternates responsibilities and swaps chores on a weekly or monthly basis.

Privacy is another problem. It is important that all parties reach an agreement concerning privacy and the need to preserve one's own space. This may mean maintaining a separate savings or checking account, taking time away by oneself on occasion for visiting friends or family or for vacation or leisure activities, or for a woman, keeping a previous surname for personal or professional reasons. Obviously, if a woman does opt to change her name it will involve a good deal of paperwork: changing her driver's license, credit cards, social security card, will, passport, and magazine subscriptions, to name only a few items. Again, recognizing and talking through these matters calmly and honestly prior to the marriage is a great way to head off a major conflict down the line.

In recent years many couples have found it helpful to draw up a marriage contract specifying the terms of their new living arrangement. If a death, separation, or divorce should occur, the spouse and children will already have settled on such matters as the disposition of personal goods, real estate, and money. But even if no formal contract is drawn up (some would consider it just too unromantic!), there is real value in discussing and settling such matters before remarrying.

In the end, the formula for ensuring success in beginning a new household is open communication and shared responsibility. This is particularly true in today's culture, when so many women are working full time in the marketplace. Today, the average woman working a steady job also works close to five hours a day at home: cooking, cleaning, and laundering, to say nothing of caring for a husband and children. Since this overextension can take a burdensome and unfair toll on the woman, her husband must either pitch in and do a fair share of the household and child-rearing tasks or else risk engendering a feeling in his wife and children that he doesn't care for them enough to spend time doing things with and for them.

In the past, men tended to see their roles rather clearly. A man was the breadwinner, the head of the household who commanded respect and was the defender of home and hearth. A man was expected to be a high achiever, career oriented, the leader in initiating the sexual relationship, yet emotionally non-demonstrative. On the other hand, women were oppositely pigeonholed as being made for fulfilling men, as the lyrics of "As Time Goes By" ran: "Woman needs man, and man must have his mate." Women were to be nurturing, motherly homemakers; their role was to please their mates, be subservient to and rely on them, and be the heart of the household, emotionally expressive and not too intellectually inclined. Such stereotypes shortchange the full human potential of both men and women and seem no longer valid in our day. A more liberated approach to both men's and women's roles seems necessary if remarriage is to be fruitful.

Setting up a new household is never an easy affair. But a willingness to talk and to listen and to compromise along the way can make for a smoother and more satisfying transition— one that can last a lifetime.

20

FINANCIAL MATTERS

Money matters are a main concern for anyone who is married or preparing to marry. Psychologists and marriage counselors say that many marital conflicts are prompted by financial problems, including misunderstandings over how to use money. Because of the complex nature of second marriages, these difficulties can be even more troublesome for couples contemplating such marriages. They are well advised to spend a good deal of time talking over money matters before beginning their new life together. They should focus on both general attitudes and on the particular ways they will earn and spend the anticipated income. And the couple should openly discuss financial matters throughout the course of their marriage, especially when income shrinks or when expenditures significantly increase.

It is extremely important for the couple to learn how each feels about money management. Since they may have developed very different attitudes toward this in their youth or in a previous marriage, this is a critical area in which the partners should freely express their attitudes and feelings. Each person is wise to listen carefully to the aspirations and dreams of the other and to seek to understand the life-style the other wishes to maintain. Some clear agreement should be reached before the marriage, since the attitudes, feelings, and actions of the couple concerning money are a pivotal factor in determining how well they will weather the storms that will inevitably come.

The couple need to take inventory and analyze their financial situation. It may require getting together a number of times to discuss and outline financial plans so as to head off potential problems. They should reflect carefully on what transpires during such sessions and should devote particular attention to any areas of conflict. Such meetings are intended to produce new insights for both persons and to allow for a comfortable resolution of potential conflicts. If some prolonged disagreement or bitter conflict should surface, the couple should seek competent premarital counseling. The conversation might center on such matters as budgeting, savings, and investments, whether or not both parties will work, where the family intends to live, what kind of strain housing costs will place on their resources, and who will manage the money. They must also consider the future educational and occupational goals of each of the spouses, whether or not each will require an automobile, what they expect to spend for food, clothing, and entertainment, and how the household will be decorated and furnished.

As the couple reflect on their attitudes toward money and consider some of the financial burdens they will face, they need to balance their planning by realistically assessing both their assets and their liabilities. To assess what their combined worth will be, they can total up their cash on hand, savings, securities or money market funds, insurance, guaranteed step-increments in income, various kinds of property, and so forth, and then compare these total assets against the projected rate of inflation, any outstanding debts owed through overdue bills, time payments, or unpaid loans, along with the cost of moving to a new household and whatever other expenses they incur for the wedding and honeymoon. After taking stock of both assets and liabilities, the couple can determine what their fixed expenses are, such as rent or mortgage payments, insurance premiums, and monthly utility and transportation expenses. Then they will be in a position to gauge how much they will need to break even. They will have begun to set up a system for dealing with financial concerns and will have to agree upon who will handle the money, pay the bills, and be responsible for earmarking a set percentage of the income for savings.

This kind of planning is called budgeting. Even before the marriage, the couple can begin to keep track of all income and expenses for three to six months in order to set up a realistic basis for planning. If the plan arrived at is inflexible and not workable, it will never take hold, and the couple will lack the motivation to carry it through. Partners who commit themselves to sound principles of financial management seek to see things in light of a monthly plan. By keeping accurate records of all expenditures, they can have a running check on the budget plan and be able to make any necessary adjustments to bring it back into line with realistic figures.

Perhaps the best financial advice for a couple preparing for remarriage is: Check out the cost of things with people who have been through the experience (relatives, friends, or acquaintances), especially those who fall into the same income range and who are accustomed to the same life-style. Note, too, that many insurance companies and banks provide useful pamphlets on budgeting that are a good starting point. Used wisely, a budget will enhance the sense of security of a marriage and help to create a more promising future for all concerned. If the subject of money is approached honestly and diligently, budget planning can take the edge out of much marital anxiety, stretch out the value of a couple's earnings, and offer a strong degree of peace of mind, because the spouses know that expenses can be met and bills paid on time. A budget can be the lifeline of a marriage, the ticket to its economic survival. To do without one is to court disaster.

A pitfall for many married couples is how to use credit. If the couple decide to make a major purchase by borrowing rather than drawing on savings, they will need a realistic sense of how much they can afford to pay back on a regular basis over the time for which the item is financed. It is always good to do some comparative shopping to obtain the best possible rate, taking into consideration the size of the down payment and the number of months allotted to repay the loan. Often, couples who buy on credit get in over their heads. It is important to keep in mind that whether the credit is extended through a bank or finance-company loan, installment payments, or the use of charge cards, credit is never free.

It is important that the couple realize they are paying for a service when they buy things on credit. They need to be aware of how much more they are paying in the long run to purchase something on time rather than with cash, since credit translates into dollars and cents. Only then can they make a realistic decision as to whether it makes sense to buy now and pay later. At times there may be definite advantages to deferring payments and buying on credit, while at other times it makes better sense to save the money and pay cash. For some, using the "plastic money" of credit cards disguises what they are actually spending and sometimes encourages a buying spree that can throw a couple into debt for months or years to come. In dealing with credit, the old axiom holds true: "Let the buyer beware."

Another major financial matter for a couple to agree upon is insurance coverage. There are many different types of insurance: health, life, homeowner or renter, fire, and automotive, to name the most common ones. While the premiums for such policies may take a major bite out of a family's budget, the coverage they provide is an economic necessity for most households in today's financial climate. Often, large companies will offer their employees and their employees' families free health (and perhaps, life) insurance coverage. But if such benefits are lacking or inadequate, then the couple should seek expanded coverage. Considering the present-day rates for a hospital stay or the replacement costs for a home or automobile, the couple risk financial disaster by not protecting themselves and their household adequately.

A final item centers on the question of making a will—a written document by which a person provides for the disposition of his or her goods and property, effective at the time of death. Such a document can be revoked, changed completely, or amended at any time. But if there is no will, the courts will dispose of one's property according to structures established by state law. Making a will can help to save estate taxes, avoid unnecessary delay in probate courts, and eliminate the impersonal and arbitrary disposition of property by the state—a process that may deprive one's family or friends of a fuller share of the estate.

It is beneficial in many ways to make and maintain an up-to-date will. A will can offer a person the peace of mind that comes from knowing that his or her estate will be distributed according to his or her stated intentions. Naming a capable executor and a trustee and/or guardian ensures the ongoing care of the surviving family. It minimizes certain costs of probating the estate, and earmarks the necessary cash to pay immediate expenses and debts. It specifies favorite charities as beneficiaries, and denotes the specific amount that each beneficiary will receive. A will often saves survivors the hassles of time, energy, and money that court-ordered settlements consume when a will is lacking.

If young children are involved, the will may name a person to act as a trustee or guardian to arrange for the management of funds until the children attain their majority. A guardian arranges for the personal care of the children, while a trustee oversees any money left to them. Testators (will-makers) should consult a competent attorney, who will translate their desire into legal language so that in the future there will be certitude about their intentions. An attorney can offer advice and counsel, but the testators should specify how they want to dispose of their property. In the end, these are highly personal decisions that only the testators themselves can make.

Obviously, money matters are a complex and tricky aspect of marriage and family life. There are no easy formulas or infallibly "right" solutions for settling differences or resolving difficulties that couples encounter when they marry again. But if they are committed to maintaining a careful, prudent, and realistic pattern of spending and are willing to save, to budget their money, and to seek outside help from financial experts when problems develop, then they are off to a good start.

If one or both partners have been previously married, then there are a number of special factors to consider. A man may have to continue paying child support or alimony, and this may siphon off as much as 20% to 40% of his paycheck. If both parties have been financially independent for a while, they may choose to maintain separate savings or checking accounts. If both spouses are working, they may want to settle on a formula for allocating their salaries equitably, particularly if one earns significantly more than the other. Some marriage counselors suggest that each party contribute a fixed percentage of his or her income to cover household expenses. This may be adjusted to take into account such factors as child support and alimony payments, but the money left over should be considered as each person's private spending money for clothing, entertainment, recreational or leisure activities, or whatever.

Many previously married couples quickly point out that they are far more reticent to merge money completely the second time around. This does not necessarily reflect a lack of confidence in the prospects for their new marriage, but rather stems from the fact that each partner has already learned to be responsible for his or her own finances, either in the previous marriage or in the time between marriages. In light of this, couples entering a second marriage should be ready to show more flexibility on financial matters in the new union. In many ways, in the long run, they are more likely to find this a far more agreeable arrangement.

21

FAMILY PLANNING

For those to whom child-bearing remains a possibility, a major issue that calls for discussion prior to remarriage is the question of openness to children, and at what intervals. Just about anyone who has been married has some feelings about children, and if the intended spouse has already had children by a previous marriage, he or she may have particularly strong feelings in this matter. Since such feelings generally do not go away or lessen with time or marriage, if one spouse ardently desires children while the other doesn't they would be well advised to grapple with the topic beforehand and to seek out premarital counseling in order to head off difficulties.

The questions surrounding family planning and the regulation of birth are important ones in almost any marriage, particularly when one or both of the partners are Catholic, since the Church in its official teaching spells out a rather clear posture. In 1968, Pope Paul VI issued a controversial encyclical letter, *Humanae Vitae* ("Of Human Life"), which condemned artificial means of contraception and restated the position that "each and every marriage act must remain open to the transmission of life" (no. 11). This stance was echoed by Pope John Paul II on his visit to the United States. Speaking to the American bishops in Chicago on October 5, 1979, he said, "In exalting the beauty of marriage you rightly spoke against both the ideology of contraception and contraceptive acts, as did the Encyclical *Humanae Vitae,* and I myself today, with the same conviction of Paul VI, ratify the teaching of the Encyclical. . . ."

Almost from the moment of its appearance, *Humanae Vitae* drew a firestorm of criticism from laity, pastors, and theologians alike, especially within the American Catholic community. While there was much reaction and overreaction to the encyclical on both sides of the debate that raged in the United States and throughout the world, it should be borne in mind that Paul was sincerely seeking to express the most ideal moral response available to Catholics concerning means of regulating birth. In certain ways, the strength of Paul's position has been vindicated somewhat in recent years as researchers demonstrate negative complications and side effects of such artificial means of contraception as the birth-control pill and the I.U.D. (intra-uterine device) and also report the refinement of a comparably reliable and "natural" option in the Billings Method.

However, even in light of these historical twists, the fact remains that an astounding number of Catholic faithful (and perhaps an almost equal proportion of their priests) have parted from the officially stated moral ideal outlined in recent papal teaching on artificial forms of contraception. One indication of this is reflected in the findings of a recent survey conducted at Princeton University, which showed that 76.5% of all American Catholic women use some form of birth control, and further, that 94% of those women use methods condemned by *Humanae Vitae*. A study by the National Opinion Research Center indicates that 70% of all parish priests support the conscience decision of a couple to engage in some form of artificial contraception if that decision is warranted by some serious pastoral reason. In the judgment of many priests, if a husband and wife were confronted with some serious medical, financial, or emotional difficulty and could not, in conscience, agree to conceive a child for the foreseeable future, they might conclude that their need for and right to the essential human-Christian values expressed in conjugal love would justify their use of artificial methods of birth control. If this decision were arrived at in good conscience and with a genuine concern for the well-being and education of present and future children and for maintaining essential human and Christian values within the family, then the action of the couple might be considered objectively morally justified, these priests assert.

One of the often-perceived shortcomings of the teaching reflected in *Humanae Vitae* is that its argument excessively emphasizes the physiological aspects of the marriage act, while by contrast many professional theologians and members of the laity alike now insist that the meaning of human actions must be found in the total person, not in some isolated aspect of the person. A refreshingly different approach to these issues was taken by Cardinal Basil Hume of London at the Synod of World Bishops' meeting in the fall of 1980, where he stated:

> It is well known that the whole question of birth control has been in recent years controversial, and the well-being of the Church has suffered.
>
> People have reacted differently. Some have no difficulty in accepting the total prohibition of the use of artificial contraception; . . . others cannot accept the total prohibition of the use of artificial contraception where circumstances seem to make this [practice] necessary or even desirable. Natural methods of birth control do not seem to them to be the definitive and only solution. It cannot just be said that these persons have failed to overcome their human frailty and weakness. The problem is more complex than that. Indeed, such persons are often good, conscientious and faithful sons and daughters of the Church. They just cannot accept that the use of artificial means of contraception is "intrinsically dishonest," as the latter [term] has been generally understood.

It would seem that the major point to be considered on this issue is the question of *responsible* transmission of life in marriage, a concern that entails a basic readiness and capacity to respond to God's gifts and call. But the bottom line is that it is the primary responsibility of the spouses to discuss and decide together how many children they want and at what intervals. In the end only they can make this decision, by taking into account the depth of their mutual love, their physical and mental health, and their ability to educate and nurture children within their communion of life and love in marriage. While great care needs to be taken to ensure that this criterion does not backslide into selfishness or hedonism, many contemporary Catholic moral theologians insist that the decision of the couple is ultimately a matter of personal consciences and that no priest, doctor, or counselor can make that decision for them.

A very positive encapsulated approach to this understanding of responsible parenthood is contained in Vatican II's *Pastoral Constitution of the Church in the Modern World* (sometimes known by its Latin title, *Gaudium et Spes*):

> Parents should regard as their proper mission the task of transmitting human life and educating those to whom it has been transmitted. They should realize that they are thereby cooperators with the love of God the Creator, and are, so to speak, interpreters of that love. Thus they will fulfill that task with human and Christian responsibility. With docile reverence towards God, they will come to the right decision by common counsel and effort. They will thoughtfully take into account both their own welfare and that of their children, those already born and those which may be foreseen. For this accounting they will reckon with both the material and spiritual conditions of the times as well as of their state in life. Finally, they will consult the interest of their family group, of temporal society, and of the Church herself. The parents themselves should ultimately make this judgment, in the sight of God. (no. 50)

This key emphasis on parental responsibility found further articulation in Pope Paul VI's 1967 Encycylical *Populorum Progressio* ("On the Development of Peoples"), in which he noted plainly: "Parents themselves must decide how many children to have. Parents themselves must consider their responsibilities before God and before each other, before their present children and before the community. Parents themselves must follow their consciences, formed by the law of God" (no. 37).

It remains part of the teaching mission of the Church to give witness to the ideals of fruitful and responsible love, but the realm of conscience has come to the fore as the major consideration in this area for couples contemplating or having entered marriage. The centrality of conscience was outlined clearly by Pope John Paul II just a few months before his election as pope, while he addressed a conference in Milan marking the tenth anniversary of the encyclical *Humanae Vitae*. In his keynote address, the then-Cardinal Wojtyla urged:

The pivot of the whole matter is the conscience. It is self-evident that in all other fields of morality conscience is also in the final analysis the decisive factor, and the value of human deeds depends upon it directly, but in this chapter of morality conscience becomes the crucial point in a particular fashion. We are here in the sphere of a type of action and cooperation, in which two people, a man and a woman, remain totally alone with each other, thrown upon what they are, not only in their physical masculinity and femininity, but also in their interior experiencing of each other, in that experience which of its nature is of an intimate character, hidden from the world and from the judgment of others. In such a situation, one's own conscience seems particularly decisive: an upright and mature conscience, a conscience both human and Christian will indicate here and now the proper measure of responsibility. "The parents themselves should ultimately make this judgment, in the sight of God," we read in *Gaudium et Spes* (no. 50). Responsibility for love and responsibility for parenthood may finally be reduced to the many judgments of the conscience of the husband and wife.

At times this judgment may bring the Catholic party or couple into conflict with the official teaching of the Church. However, it should be recognized that the hierarchical teaching office of the Church is not the only way in which the community of faith teaches and learns, and that much may be gained by seriously considering the "sense of the faithful" and recognizing that the Spirit works at the grassroots of the Church as well as at its upper echelons.

As Pope John Paul pointed out in the Milan address, the pivot of the entire matter is conscience. The formation of and attentiveness to one's conscience is one of the most important and delicate aspects of second-marriage preparation, and it requires careful consideration in a book such as this. What, then, is conscience? From the Catholic perspective, it is a unique human faculty that judges the morality of individual actions according to recognized ethical principles. Christian conscience is the experience of ourselves as new creatures in Christ, enlightened by the Holy Spirit. In one of the most beautiful and profound statements of the Second Vatican Council, in the *Pastoral Constitution of the Church in the Modern World,* the nature of Christian conscience was outlined:

> To obey it is the very dignity of man; according to it he will be judged.
>
> Conscience is the most secret core and sanctuary of a man. There he is alone with God, whose voice echoes in his depths. In a wonderful manner conscience reveals that law which is fulfilled by love of God and neighbor. In fidelity to conscience, Christians are joined with the rest of men in the search for truth, and for the genuine solution to the numerous problems which arise in the life of individuals and from social relationships. Hence the more that a correct conscience holds sway, the more persons and groups turn aside from blind choice and strive to be guided by objective norms of morality.
>
> Conscience frequently errs from invincible ignorance without losing its dignity. (no. 16)

One respected contemporary Catholic moral theologian, Timothy O'Connell, sees three distinct levels of meaning in the term *conscience.* First, it is a fundamental sense of value and of personal responsibility, an intuitive ability to weigh the difference between what is right and wrong. Second, it is a means of formulating a judgment concerning the moral acceptability of a specific act, through a process of discernment and consultation. Third, it is the final norm of moral action, the decision to follow a course that one deems to be right.

But how do we form our conscience? How do we go about making conscience decisions? To follow the old adage, "Let your conscience be your guide" is certainly not enough. Consciences need to be more than sincere, well intentioned. For moral issues can be very complex and can demand knowledge and wisdom drawn from many sources. Consciences need to be well informed; they need objective norms to follow in order to avoid the dangers of error and unconscious self-deception. In short, moral problems can be so difficult that it is almost impossible for any one person to be sufficiently knowledgeable and responsible without seeking outside help and guidance.

What are these outside sources of moral guidance and wisdom? There are many: the broad range of human experience, scientific knowledge, the Scriptures, the Church. The Church stands out as an indispensable guide because of her life of faith, varied history, breadth of experience and worldwide resources that cut across temporal and cultural barriers, and above all because the Holy Spirit is especially present within her to guide and enlighten her. Hence, the Church plays an important role in helping to form the conscience of individual Christians by teaching, supporting, challenging, and questioning them and by guiding them to a deeper maturity in faith so they can make conscientious moral choices, free from the likelihood of self-deception or rationalization.

The wisdom of the faith community expressed in moral norms serves to enlighten conscience, but never replaces it. Conscience itself is ultimately dependent upon and is brought together by what is called the practice of discernment as one probes one's own heart and soul and that of the community to see which movements or impulses are truly the work of the Holy Spirit. Discernment is the gift of being able to separate out those things that are of God from those that are not. As

St. John wrote, "Beloved, do not trust every spirit, but put the spirits to a test to see if they belong to God . . . we distinguish the spirit of truth from the spirit of deception" (1 John 4:1,6b). St. Paul encouraged the early Christians in a similar vein: "Do not stifle the spirit. . . . Test everything; retain what is good" (1 Thessalonians 5:19,21).

One can be authentically discerning only when rooted in a prayerful union with God. As Father Philip Keane points out:

> Only in such prayerfulness can the narrow biases of individuals and communities be overcome, and particular discernments will be more or less successful to the degree of openness to the Lord from which they spring. This does not mean that discernment can be made into a short-cut around the hard work of analysis that must enter into moral choices. But in a theological perspective, a God-oriented attitude is the most basic requirement for decision-making. (*Sexual Morality: A Catholic Perspective.* New York: Paulist Press, 1977, p. 56)

How does a person square his or her conscience with authentic but non-infallible moral teaching of the Church? The faithful Catholic will respond to such teaching with religious assent of mind and will. (Into this category fall all official pronouncements that have not been clearly designated as infallible.) By its very nature, non-infallible teaching is fallible. Hence it calls for a conditional response, since the possibility of error and of revision exists. But in spite of certain limitations marking the Church's teaching office (the magisterium), a faithful Catholic will always consider and respect the moral teachings of the Church before arriving at a conscience decision. This principle is well expressed by the noted Jesuit moral theologian Richard McCormick:

> Such openness and readiness will translate into respect for the teacher and his office, a willingness to reassess one's own position, a reluctance to conclude error on the part of the teacher, behavior in the public sphere which

fosters respect for the teacher. If one brings these qualities to the non-infallible teachings of the magisterium, he has responded proportionately to the authority of the teacher. It is in this sense that the ethical teaching of the magisterium can be said to be binding on the Catholic conscience. ("Personal Conscience," in *An American Catholic Catechism*. New York: Seabury Press, 1978, p. 185)

In spite of the fact that most Catholics recognize their duty to pay heed to the teaching office of the Church, at times it may become reasonably clear that the Church's magisterium has failed to form its position adequately, or has perhaps even erred. In such circumstances, the possibility of responsible dissent arises. Since absolute certitude is never achievable in specific moral matters, a person may conclude, after sufficient prayer, study, and consultation, that he or she has persuasive and binding reasons for parting from an official Church teaching, and such a judgment is to be respected. This is particularly true if other competent parties have independently reached the same conclusion.

Although the Church assists couples in forming a right conscience, their conscientious moral judgments are to be respected even when they do not conform to recognized church order. A great strength of the unbroken Catholic tradition is that the conscience decisions of individual believers are what ultimately must be followed in matters of Christian morality. The Thomistic tradition held that a person with a certain conscience was bound to follow it, and St. Thomas Aquinas himself went so far as to declare, "Anyone upon whom the ecclesiastical authority, in ignorance of true facts, imposes a demand that offends against his clear conscience, should perish in excommunication rather than violate his conscience" (*IV Sentences,* dist. 38, a. 4; see also *Summa Theologica,* I-II, q. 5, a. 19).

The traditional Catholic moral norms concerning conscience hold that no one should be prevented from following even an erroneous conscience, unless the action undertaken would be seriously harmful to oneself or others. Furthermore, the Catholic tradition has consistently asserted that no one may force or persuade another to act against his or her conscience. This posture found its clearest articulation in Vatican II's *Declaration on Religious Freedom,* considered by church historians such as John Tracy Ellis to be the Council's most outstanding achievement:

> . . . (T)he demand is increasingly made that men should act on their own judgment, enjoying and making use of a responsible freedom, not driven by coercion but motivated by a sense of duty. . . .
>
> This sacred Synod likewise professes its belief that it is upon the human conscience that these obligations fall and exert their binding force. . . . (no. 1)
>
> (F)reedom means that all men are to be immune from coercion on the part of individuals or of social groups and of any human power, in such wise that in matters religious no one is to be forced to act in a manner contrary to his own beliefs. Nor is anyone to be restrained from acting in accordance with his own beliefs, whether privately or publicly, whether alone or in association with others, within due limits. . . . (no. 2)
>
> On his part, man perceives and acknowledges the imperatives of the divine law through the mediation of conscience. In all his activity a man is bound to follow his conscience faithfully, in order that he may come to know God, for whom he was created. It follows that he is not to be forced to act in a manner contrary to his conscience. Nor, on the other hand, is he to be restrained from acting in accordance with his conscience, especially in matters religious.
>
> For, of its very nature, the exercise of religious freedom consists before all else in those internal, voluntary, and free acts whereby man sets the course of his life directly toward God. No merely human power can either command or prohibit acts of this kind. (no. 3)

It is clear, then, that Catholic tradition holds for the primacy and inviolability of the individual conscience. This means that a person is obliged to do right as he or she sees the right after he or she has made a sincere and serious effort to find out what is morally right.

At times a couple may unavoidably find themselves pitted in conflict with the official posture of the Church on a given moral issue. This is particularly true in the matter of birth control, but it has bearing upon the internal forum solution and the questions of access to the sacraments as well. A brief survey of the statements of several national bishops' conferences issued in the aftermath of *Humanae Vitae* offers enlightening guidance on the Catholic stance favoring the primacy of conscience:

1. The *Belgian* bishops: "If someone competent in the matter and capable of forming a well-founded judgment—which necessarily supposes sufficient information—after serious investigation, before God, reaches different conclusions at certain points, he has the right to follow his convictions on this matter, provided that he remains disposed to continue his investigation."

2. The *Canadian* bishops: " . . . whoever honestly chooses that course that seems right to him does so in good conscience."

3. The *Dutch* bishops: " . . . many factors determine one's personal conscience regarding marriage rules, for example, mutual love, the relations in a family, and social circumstances."

4. The *German* bishops: "Pastors must respect the responsible decisions of conscience made by the faithful."

5. The *Scandinavian* bishops: "No one, including the Church, can absolve anyone from the obligation to follow his conscience. . . . If someone for weighty and well-considered reasons cannot become convinced by the argumentation of the encyclical, it has always been conceded that he is allowed to have a different view from that presented in a non-infallible statement of the Church. No one should be considered a bad Catholic because he is of such a dissenting opinion."

6. The *United States'* bishops: "There exists in the Church a lawful freedom of inquiry and of thought and also general norms of licit dissent. . . . These norms also require setting forth one's dissent with propriety and with regard for the gravity

of the matter and the deference due the authority which has pronounced it."

This consensus of many of the world's leading national bishops' conferences highlights the primacy of conscience and spells out the possibility for responsible dissent on specific moral issues such as family planning. It also serves as a reminder that there are many aspects and instruments of teaching in the Church, and that the whole Church—clergy and laity alike—is magisterial (has teaching authority). This point was clearly expressed by Bishop Basil C. Butler of London, who pointed out:

> It cannot be reasonably maintained, in the face of Vatican II, that the Church is divided into an *ecclesia docens* ["teaching Church"] consisting of the bishops and an *ecclesia discens* ["learning Church"] embracing all other baptized persons. On the contrary, everyone in the Church, from the Pope downwards, belongs to the "learning Church" and has to receive information and enlightenment from his fellow believers; and everyone in the Church who has reached maturity has, at some time or another, to play the role of the teacher, the *magister,* the *ecclesia docens.* ("Authority and the Christian Conscience," *Clergy Review* 60, January 1975, p. 13)

As we have mentioned, the main teacher in the Church is the Holy Spirit, who resides in the hearts of all believers. The Spirit acts in people's hearts to prompt them to right action and to spur them to grow in wisdom, age, and grace, as followers of Christ. If after seeking spiritual counsel and seriously examining the issue before God and each other a couple come to a conclusion at odds with the official teaching of the Church on a moral issue, as so many have in recent years on the matter of birth control, they need to do so respectfully, be aware of the dangers of compromising the common good of the community and of the human family, and above all sincerely seek the best Christian way of responding in the concrete circumstances of their own marriage and family lives, while constantly remaining open to the possibility of a better response. They should always have serious, well-founded reasons for such dissent, since such issues affect not only the "domestic church" of this particular family but also the larger community of faith as well. The couple need to allow sufficient time for prayerful reflection and discernment. In that way, the tendency to be self-deceiving or self-serving will find ample checks and balances, and an honest response will take form, one with which the couple can live in integrity and peace.

22

UNDERSTANDING THE STAGES
OF MARRIAGE

In the late 1970s, drugstore counters, supermarket checkout lines, and newsstand bookracks throughout the country overflowed with copies of Gail Sheehy's runaway bestseller, *Passages,* a popular account of the distinct stages and crisis points through which people pass as they move into adulthood and middle age. Sheehy borrowed much of her material freely from the work of Yale psychologist Daniel Levinson and his associates, which Levinson later published under the title of *The Seasons of a Man's Life.* The basic insight of Levinson's work is that persons pass through an underlying pattern of adult life stages that can be predictably charted and that bring with them certain important choices and consequences. Each of these "seasons" of a person's life brings with it periods of both traumatic upheaval and even-keeled consistency, depending upon the nature of the life choices the person is making at that particular moment.

Levinson divides the adult life cycle into six stages, each lasting about seven years (his study did not cover old age):

1. the early adult transition (17-22);
2. entrance into the adult world (22-28);
3. the age-thirty transition (28-33);
4. the time of settling down (33-40);
5. the mid-life transition (40-45);
6. the period of middle adulthood (45-60).

Levinson views marriage as a major event that is influenced by and contributes greatly to each stage. While he recognizes that most people seek to maintain a long-term relationship and to form and raise a family while in their twenties, he asserts that at this point most persons simply aren't ready to make the kind of enduring and permanent inner commitment to spouse and family that marriage requires: ". . . they are not capable of a highly loving, sexually free, and emotionally intimate relationship" (*The Seasons of a Man's Life,* p. 107).

By the time a person reaches the "age-thirty transition," he or she may have felt the crunch of marital erosion or failure. If a marriage is to make it, Levinson says, it needs a strong commonality in background and levels of interest: in age, educational level and income, willingness to respect the other's need for independence and autonomy, ability to convey affection and esteem, and desire and ability to share freely and openly in personal interests and on the sexual level. It would seem that, for many couples, the prospects are weighted from the very beginning against their marriage making it unless there is such a degree of commonality. Levinson also observes that there is little proof to support the theory that complementary needs or traits contribute to marital happiness. While opposites may attract initially, they may not hold together well over the course of time. During the period of change around the age of thirty, the spouses experience much questioning and reevaluation as they seek to work out the flaws and limitations in their designs for living, and explore the possibilities for change. Significantly, this is the time when many extramarital affairs, separations, and divorces occur. It is a time when persons try to take stock, individually and as a married couple, of where they have been and where they are going. If there appears to be a cause for dissatisfaction in the relationship, this is a point when the partners may begin to turn away from each other and build more distance into their relationship, while seeking elsewhere for satisfaction of their needs.

At this point the couple may discover that their marriage is quite different from what they had supposed it would be. At this time, or in the later thirties, a man may become greatly dissatisfied with his marriage. He may struggle to assert his masculinity more and to seek the more external affirmations of society, especially if he feels that his wife regards him as a boy. In some ways he may perceive her as excessively controlling or smothering, and he may therefore seek out another woman whom he finds more understanding, open, or sexually attractive. This may prompt him to try to "break out" of the marriage bond by seeking a divorce and possibly remarrying, or by working out an arrangement whereby both his wife and a sexual partner on the side figure in his life. Often the man will shift the blame for any problems onto his wife rather than admit any responsibility for them. While he may eventually lay to rest his illusions concerning his wife and his marital relationship, he may find it unpleasant to come to terms with his illusions about himself.

If the marital relationship weathers the storm of the age-thirty transition, as the couple moves into the settling-down phase it is often the wife who takes charge in reappraising the marriage. A number of factors influence this "settling-down period" (33-40), and they can place pressure on a marriage. While for some persons this is a time in which deep roots are sunk in family, others may concentrate more outside the household on jobs or forms of community service in order to be able to take pride in their accomplishments and realize their ambitions, values, and dreams. During this time marital satisfaction is diminished and the marital relationship is pushed into second place. There are many additional pressures at work during this phase. The children can become the focus of the spouses' attention and can therefore become the primary object of their affection. Unresolved sexual difficulties and unmet sexual needs can linger and take a further toll on the marriage. The normal strains of parenthood and especially of raising adolescent children can combine to further erode the bond between the spouses.

It seems that at this point the wife in particular shapes the direction of the marriage as she becomes freer of family responsibilities and seeks to broaden her horizons and undertake new activities outside the confines of the home. At this juncture the wife often becomes the symbol of development and change.

Her growth and the new directions she has undertaken may pose a threat to her husband, who fears the loss of his youthfulness and sees the balance of their relationship upset in her favor. At times the growing freedom and assertiveness of the wife can set off an accompanying decline of ego strength on her husband's part as he perceives himself to be less independent and to have less authority in the structure of the family. This unfolding pattern is especially severe when coupled with the common feeling of being outmoded or obsolete on the job. If these things occur, they have a ripple effect on the whole family and may place the marriage in serious jeopardy.

The next stage the couple may experience is the period of the "mid-life transition" (from 40-45). Ordinarily, this is a time to take stock of the direction one's life has taken and to reassess and reevaulate oneself as person, spouse, and parent. Here the spouses may begin to set limits for themselves and to come to terms realistically with the evolving changes that have marked each other. For some, the profound physical changes (menopause, signs of aging, or diminished sexual drive, for instance) may channel the person into a frantic pattern of denial and escape, marked by workaholic tendencies, drug and alcohol abuse, extramarital affairs, or extreme depression. Others, however, react differently to the changes in their marriage and family life, and the crisis can allow the spouses to assume a greater degree of responsibility for their marriage and to use this time to work through new levels of growth in marital intimacy. As the spouses continue to pass through this stage, they may be less inclined to heap blame upon each other and be more disposed to "own" the situation and come to terms with their own responsibilities in keeping up the relationship.

The final passage that Levinson sketches out is the period of "middle adulthood" (from 45 to 60). For couples who make it this far, this is a time for more self-reflection and greater freedom for hobbies and leisure activities, a time for venturing into broader outlets of service and community-oriented activities, developing wider networks of friends, and learning to relate more maturely to spouse, children, and others. In general, this is a time for more gentle, mature togetherness as the couple prepares for retirement and perhaps for their new role as grandparents. As they grow older they may well continue to discover the depth of the personal qualities that they can share with the other—their strengths and weaknesses, gifts and needs.

The pioneering work of Levinson and his associates is a useful means for becoming aware that every marital relationship can expect to run into periods of calm and stability but also periods of turbulence, particularly as it moves through the "passages" of each person's life. Being aware of such possibilities and being willing to work to overcome both the predictable and the unexpected stresses that face every married couple can help head off disaster and can transform the crisis points into occasions for building stronger, healthier marriage bonds.

23

ONGOING MARRIAGE ENRICHMENT AND CONFLICT RESOLUTION

There is a familiar ring to the ending of so many children's stories and fairy tales: "They were married and lived happily ever after." But common experience tells us that no couple survive the seasons of their marriage untouched by conflict. When the balance of a marriage is disturbed, conflict sets in, as one (or perhaps both) of the spouses feels that he or she is giving more to the relationship than the other person is, and that the benefits derived from the marriage no longer outweigh the costs incurred in the day-to-day interchange. Marital conflict can escalate rapidly as external events trigger confrontations between the spouses. Such encounters can result in resolution of the difficulties or in further alienation and distancing.

The most common areas of marital stress and conflict are money management, division of household tasks, the process of decision-making, goals and values, and leisure-time pursuits. Sexual incompatibility and the need for affection, touch, and stroking can also provoke conflict, as do many aspects of parenting, association with family, friends or in-laws, drug and alcohol use, and different religious, social, and political outlooks. Even marriages "made in heaven" have to struggle to make it on earth. If conditions are ripe, many factors can prompt a clash between spouses that escalates to full-blown warfare, particularly if they involve the areas just mentioned.

In the past, family therapists tended to see marital conflicts as a result of interlocking neuroses afflicting the couple. That is, they felt that some unresolved emotional problem initially drew the couple together, then surfaced later as a major cause of their inability to relate well together. The counselor would interview each spouse separately, to help each understand and begin to work through his or her own inner problems. The increasingly more common approach today is not to assign fault for the breakdown in the relationship to either of the spouses, but rather to view their inability to function together as a failure in basic interaction and teamwork. This view focuses on adjusting the *process* of interaction more than on improving the psychodynamics of the individuals. In other words, a growing number of marital therapists believe that the problem with most hurting couples does not rest within either or both partners but in the contradictory rules and the self-defeating patterns of behavior that get in the way of their healthy interaction and teamwork.

It is not always obvious to a couple that each one is following his or her own set of rules, acquired by growing up in different families, by having been exposed to different role models, or by experiencing different personal histories and accepting different values and priorities. In such cases the couple must recognize their potential areas of conflict and learn how to communicate better with each other, especially in expessing their feelings more effectively.

The couple need to learn positive rules for communication, such as hearing the other person out, listening carefully to what is being said, and checking out one's own and the other's feelings and perceptions. They need to learn how to negotiate disagreements, how to bargain fairly and amicably and trade things off, and how to agree on ways of resolving differences. To do these things they must follow some essential ground rules. For instance, the couple can resolve not to scream at each other or to withdraw and sulk, since both these responses are attempts to get one's way that serve to hinder or altogether destroy the possibility for constructive solutions. The way they communicate is a key to conflict management, and the words, intonations, and gestures they use can either build or wreck the relationship. In the course of time they should be able to recognize self-defeating patterns of behavior so that they can replace the styles of harmful interaction with sustaining patterns of beneficial behavior.

In order to head off or resolve conflicts, the couple must really want to change, and both partners must be committed to growth. They must be willing to develop more effective communication skills and to resolve conflicts in a positive, constructive vein.

In short, the heart of marital conflict is the spouses' inability to communicate skillfully. If they can identify problem areas as they arise within each person and are willing to negotiate with each other, they are on the right track to conflict resolution. They need to be in touch with their respective and mutual needs, desires, and expectations, and to be able to accept and deal with a certain amount of frustration, disappointment, and hurt, since no marriage is perfect, and there are bound to be some snags.

It has been said that the best marriage counseling is self-counseling. But at times a couple may come to realize that they are in over their heads and cannot bring about effective change by themselves. Any counseling experience will be futile unless the couple are willing to invest significantly in the process and to work on improving their communication and conflict-resolution skills. Effective therapy usually involves both spouses at the same time, since having only one partner in counseling can aggravate rather than minimize the problem.

The role of the counselor is to act like a mirror to the couple, to reflect back to them elements of their marriage so that they can see and begin to understand things from a new perspective. It is the task of the counselor to encourage the couple to set goals, make decisions together, carry out new plans, and change or modify unproductive ways of relating.

When should a couple seek out professional help? When the problem is too deeply rooted to be dealt with by the couple themselves or too tied into a severe personality problem, they probably need outside help. When they are so bogged down in their problems that they cannot budge or show some flexibility to each other, or if their every communication is choked off by hostility, they should seek competent counseling. If they cannot grasp the root of their problem without external assistance, or if after some initial progress they have been stymied when faced with the cause of their difficulties, they need a prudent counselor. If the marriage has degenerated to the point that either spouse feels he or she must resort to a dramatic, grandstand gesture to get the other's attention, like moving out of the house, becoming physically violent, or threatening suicide, then professional counseling is in order.

The question then arises: How do we choose a therapist? Since there are quacks and charlatans masquerading as competent marriage counselors, it is vitally important that the couple do some initial legwork to find someone who will serve their needs well. It is a good idea to get the names of two or three effective marriage counselors. But how? Word-of-mouth referrals from friends, relatives, or co-workers who share common values and preferences usually provide good leads. A respected professional (a doctor, lawyer, or priest, for instance) is usually connected with a network of therapists and should be able to recommend one or two good ones. A phone call to a non-profit social agency such as Catholic Charities could turn up something fruitful. Or, for the price of a postage stamp, one can obtain a listing of affiliated therapists working in a local area by writing one of the following agencies or associations:

1. American Association of Sex Educators, Counselors, and Therapists
   5010 Wisconsin Ave. N.W.
   Washington, DC 20016
2. American Association of Marriage and Family Counselors
   225 Yale Ave.
   Claremont, CA 91711
3. National Council of Family Relations
   1219 University Ave. S.E.
   Minneapolis, MN 55414

4. American Association of Pastoral Counselors
   3 W. 29th St.
   New York City, NY 10001
5. National Federation of Catholic Charities
   1346 Connecticut Ave. N.W.
   Washington, DC 20036

After getting the names of several counselors, the couple should set up an initial interview. During the first brief encounter, they should mention who recommended them to the therapist and should describe their problem as clearly as possible. It is important to ask when an actual counseling arrangement could begin and find out about the fee scale and arrangement for payment, as well as how long the sessions will last. As clients, the couple have a right to ask about the counselor's credentials (his or her educational background and professional affiliations), and they definitely should do so. At the close of the initial meeting the couple should ask themselves how each felt about the counselor. Was there a comfortable rapport between them? Did the therapist seem interested and engaged with them, or withdrawn and uncaring? When they have found a mutually agreeable counselor they should work out a plan detailing the frequency of the sessions and the agenda of each meeting.

The couple should be aware that they are making a serious commitment to each other by entering into the counseling relationship, and should promise that they will faithfully attend each session. They should expect to do some "homework" at times by reflecting on their situation and bringing their personal agenda and the needs of the relationship into a clearer focus.

The therapist's role is to help the couple to function better, both as individuals and as partners in the marriage relationship. The therapist will attempt to get the facts of the situation by checking out the individual and marital histories of each of the spouses and then trying to recognize and deal with the areas of trouble that have erupted. His or her task is to keep the focus on and to confront the real problems, beginning first with the more manageable ones. He or she will model for the couple a pattern by which they can communicate and differ constructively and will show them that elements of their behavior can be modified and positive changes achieved if the couple are motivated to work for change in the relationship.

Couples who do not commit themselves to ongoing growth and enrichment court potential disaster in their relationship. Fortunately, many different forms and varieties of marriage enrichment are available. Most take place either in small groups that meet over the course of six to eight weeks or continuously for an intensive weekend experience.

Probably the most famous (and successful) marriage renewal experience is Marriage Encounter. Founded in 1962 in Spain, the Marriage Encounter movement is divided into two expressions, Worldwide and National Marriage Encounter. Its primary aim is to promote increased dialogue and communication of feelings between spouses; it is not a therapy group for "problem" marriages. During a weekend a priest and a team of well-trained couples give talks on married life and love, after which the spouses separate to put down their reflections in notebooks. Each couple then return to their private rooms to share their reflections between themselves. Improved communication is the key to all the dynamics of the Marriage Encounter weekend.

Each spouse is encouraged to continue keeping a notebook journal after the weekend has concluded, and to pick his or her own prime time for writing down feelings and concerns to share with the partner. Spouses spend ten minutes each day writing in the journal, and ten more exchanging notebooks and discussing their contents. Many couples attest that the daily practice of "10 and 10" fosters a progressive growth of love, understanding, and acceptance within oneself and with the other.

The partner-in-dialogue techniques of Marriage Encounter have indeed proved successful, and are described at length in Antoinette Bosco's fine little book, *Marriage Encounter: The Rediscovery of Love* (St. Meinrad, Ind.: Abbey Press, 1972). Further information concerning its format and offerings is available through one's diocesan family life bureau or by writing directly to:

1. Worldwide Marriage Encounter (more exclusively Catholic in its approaches)
   Suite 108
   10059 Manchester Rd.
   Warson Woods, MO 63122
2. National Marriage Encounter (more open to Protestant and Jewish couples)
   5305 W. Foster Ave.
   Chicago, IL 60630

Marriage Encounter is of course not a sure-fire means of marriage enrichment, but it boasts an enviable track record. Marriage Encounter opens up many aspects of each spouse to the other. The vast majority of those who have taken part in it have been greatly enriched, and there is no firm evidence that any couples have suffered harm on account of it. On the contrary, its positive fruits have been outstanding since its introduction into the United States in the late 1960s. As one of its strongest promoters, the well-known Jesuit writer and lecturer John Powell has said, "I am sure that by and large the many couples I have known from the Marriage Encounter movement represent the happiest marriages and the happiest people I know." Techniques such as the "10 and 10" are the building blocks for making good marriages work even better.

Another popular and helpful form of couple enrichment is the Marriage Enrichment Retreat, developed by Dr. David Mace of the Association of Couples for Marriage Enrichment (ACME). ACME's aim is to help married couples express their support for successful marriage, growth, and mutual fulfillment. The format consists of a trained married couple leading five to eight other couples in weekly meetings in private homes. The spouses themselves set the agenda and spend their time together sharing experiences of their marriages with other couples and between themselves.

The Marriage Enrichment Retreat is less intensive than the forty-four hours of the Marriage Encounter weekend and has the advantage of allowing the couples more time to assimilate the dynamics of the program. If no trained leadership couples are available, a handy cassette recording entitled "How to Start a Marriage Enrichment Group" can be obtained through ACME to guide the program through the phases of its development. Further information is available by writing to: Association of Couples for Marriage Enrichment (ACME), 403 S. Hawthorne Rd., Winston-Salem, N.C. 27013.

The Marriage Encounter weekend and the Marriage Enrichment Retreat are only two of many ways of deepening the bonds of a marriage, but they are two that have proven to be very effective in the long run. Their success rests largely on carefully screened and well-trained lay leadership, built-in support systems, and follow-up procedures for downstream assistance when snags are encountered. Such programs are a very effective means for married couples to encourage, challenge, support, and learn from one another and to strengthen and enrich their relationship.

24

TOWARD A MARITAL SPIRITUALITY

In a private Journal entry, the well-known writer John Howard Griffin noted, "Theological speculation about marriage by men who have never been married always fascinates me. How rarely does it bear any resemblance to the intimate reality of the relationship between man and woman and their children! All the hearing of confessions, all the transference (of mystical love toward married love), all the 'family counseling,' etc., does not place the theologian in the sure earth of experience. . . . Usually such speculation degrades marriage in a subtle way" (*The Hermitage Journals,* Kansas City: Andrews and MacMeel, 1981, p. 131). With a certain real reticence, this celibate priest will nevertheless seek to offer some insights and reflections on the spiritual dimensions of married life, in a way that he hopes will not be too speculative or "degrading."

A spirituality of Christian marriage and family life begins with recognizing and responding to the presence of God in the ordinary moments of everyday life. It sees prayer not simply as something to be done, as an activity in life, but rather as something that people are and are caught up into by living out, in the day-to-day realities of their lives, the passage of the death and resurrection of Jesus Christ. A Christian spirituality of marriage can be seen as the process in which a couple experience the movement from sin and darkness to the warmth and light of God's freely given love. Any true spirituality has a deep sense of how God's presence and absence can serve to put the human person in touch with him. God's presence and the power of his love are manifested in many ways, especially in relationships. But the desire to know and love God is rooted in the realization that he loved us first. Getting in touch with God in prayer is not always an easy thing to do, since prayer is a place where love and pain mix. This insight is well captured by Henri Nouwen, who writes in *Reaching Out: Three Movements of the Solitary Life* (New York: Doubleday, 1975, pp. 107-108):

> To the degree that our prayer has become the prayer of our heart we will love more and suffer more, we will see more light and more darkness, more grace and more sin, more of God and more of humanity. To the degree that we have descended into our heart and reached out to God from there, solitude can speak to solitude, deep to deep, and heart to heart. It is there that love and pain are found together.

To speak of the ways in which God is revealed is to recognize that he is made known not only in his transcendent dimension but also "horizontally," in human relationships, in human love and human pain. In this sense we can speak of the sacramentality of Christian marriage as a privileged experience in which God's redeeming love is made visible to men and women. In marriage the other spouse serves as a tangible sign and mediator of our encounter with God, as a channel for communicating his presence and the power of his love. The goal of Christian marriage is to enable persons to find a place where they may experience fullness of life together, living out their Christian destiny: "I came that they might have life and have it to the full" (John 10:10).

A central insight into Christian marriage sees it as a path to spiritual reality through the discovery of persons in relationships. As the spouses come to encounter each other in depth, their marriage can become the vehicle for conveying spiritual experiences that transcend the marriage bond. To put it in a biblical perspective, they come to a personal, experiential sense that "God is love, and he who abides in love abides in God, and God in him" (1 John 4:16). In order for this kind of discovery to unfold in the relationship, the couple must learn to communicate openly, to be attentive to each other's religious convictions and needs, and to give and take in order to find a common ground where they can meaningfully pray together.

At times shared prayer can be a difficult undertaking, and many couples can readily identify with St. Paul's lament: " . . . we do not know how to pray as we ought . . . " (Romans 8:26). However, there are a number of clear and useful guidelines for growth in prayer. First, the couple must set aside some time and space so that they can reflect on the voice of God sounding in their hearts. Within each person, deeply embedded in the core of his or her being, can be felt a call to commune with God, a call poetically summed up by one of the early Fathers of the Church, St. Ignatius of Antioch: "I hear within me, as from a spring of living water, the murmur: Come to the Father." While God is consistent in the freely offered gift of himself, it is up to a person to respond and to create the time and space where he or she can respond to God's initiative. The words of Mother Teresa of Calcutta sum up the essence of prayer as a human response to God's love: "Love to pray—feel often during the day the need for prayer, and take trouble to pray. Prayer enlarges the heart until it is capable of containing God's gift of himself. Ask and seek, and your heart will grow big enough to receive him as your own."

Most persons would benefit from a few guidelines on how to pray. These three pointers almost always prove useful. First, as mentioned previously, people need quiet time and space where they can place themselves in the presence of God and tune out the distracting inner voices that obscure God's voice. It is important that this be done frequently (preferably daily) and, insofar as possible, in the presence of the other spouse. However, the attempt to listen silently for the voice of God can be misleading or illusory unless it is properly focused. For this reason the second point, the contemplative reading of Scripture, is essential if one is to reorient oneself to God's call and to draw deeper into the silence of God that in turn creates the space where the word can be heard in its full power.

The author of the Letter to the Hebrews reminds us that "God's word is living and effective, sharper than any two-edged sword. It penetrates and divides soul and spirit, joints and marrow; it judges the reflections and thoughts of the heart" (4:12). Reflective reading of the Scriptures and quiet time in the presence of the Lord are closely linked in marital spirituality, and they open a couple to the possibility of hearing and responding to God's word acting within their hearts. But both word and silence need further direction.

Spiritual guidance is the third essential feature of spiritual growth in marriage, and spouses almost always benefit from seeking out the direction of someone who is spiritually sensitive and discerning and who can help to lead them closer to God and to each other as they grow in prayer. Such guidance is not necessarily limited to a one-to-one personal encounter, though often that will be most fruitful. The time and the place in which a person lives shape and condition his or her own experience of faith, and being aware of the spiritual masters of our present day and attentive to their witness can open one up to further growth in the Lord. However, any real life experience has a universal quality about it that enables us to share across the centuries, and by drawing on the character and experience of men and women of faith like Francis and Clare, John of the Cross and Teresa of Avila, Thomas Merton and Dorothy Day, one can see what it means to live in the presence of God today.

Shared faith strengthens a marriage. Since faith is a dynamic quality that can grow or wane, couples can deepen or enrich their marriage by setting spiritual growth goals. In the course of time thay may need to develop new religious concepts and values that are meaningful to them at their respective stages of adulthood. Even in middle and advanced age, there are distinct phases through which persons pass in moral and faith development, and these transition points call for ongoing growth and revision in each spouse's personal faith and lived witness. Such activities as spiritual reading, attendance at adult religious education programs, and retreat or renewal experiences such as Genesis II or Marriage Encounter can help them to grow.

Though at first it may sound strange to traditional Catholics, one of the most important dimensions of marital spirituality is contained and expressed in sexual love. As theologian Rosemary Haughton states: " . . . sex is the 'doorway' by which love can enter and take possession of the whole personality." Sexual expression in marriage is a sign both of the couple's union and of the covenant love with Christ. It is also a pledge of the promise of eternal life, since, as Ms. Haughton adds: " . . . this love shows itself, in its beginnings, but quite really, in the mutual love and service and giving of the sexual encounter." In the sexual encounter in marriage, a couple shares in the ecstatic unitive and co-creative bonding that brings a unique depth to every level of the marital relationship. Today the Christian community more readily acknowledges the sacredness of Christian married love, as is reflected in the statement of Bishop John McGann of Rockville Centre, Long Island, in an interview celebrating the inauguration of the "Year of the Family" in 1981: "It is as sacred for a husband and wife to have intercourse in marriage as it is for a priest to celebrate the Eucharist." Christian marriage is primarily oriented toward forming and maintaining a union of life and love between the spouses, and the Chruch now more readily recognizes that sexual union can be one of the most powerful (and spiritual!) ways of achieving that end.

It is important that a married couple and their family share in the life of the larger Christian community—that their love be directed outward as well as inward. Any family's spiritual hungers are best fed at the table of the Lord in the Eucharist, where the members are nourished by word and sacrament and become more aware of the needs of the world beyond the confines of their own home. This outer dimension of Christian marriage and family life was stressed by Archbishop Jean Jadot when he commented on a pastoral plan for family ministry developed by the American Catholic bishops. He said that the plan should direct its focus on " . . . a shared experience of prayer. This finds its origins in a common reading of the Holy

Scriptures and in a concern for those who are in need, for justice and peace in the world, for the coming of the Kingdom of God. . . . Such prayer quite naturally evokes an awareness of the family's mission to service. It also raises the family's social consciousness.''

The spirituality of marriage has both its rewards and demands. It calls the partners to commit themselves to each other and to the service of others whose lives they touch. The heart of these commitments is captured by St. Paul in his Letter to the Romans:

> Your love must be sincere. Detest what is evil, cling to what is good. . . . Rejoice in hope, be patient under trial, persevere in prayer. . . .be generous in offering hospitality. . . . Have the same attitude toward all. Put away ambitious thoughts and associate with those who are lowly. Do not be wise in your own estimation. Never repay injury with injury. See that your conduct is honorable in the eyes of all. If possible, live peaceably with everyone. . . . Do not be conquered by evil but conquer evil with good. (Romans 12:9,12,13b,16-18,21)

Perhaps the greatest marital virtue, in St. Paul's words, is to ''be generous in offering hospitality.'' To offer hospitality is a way of making space in one's heart so that others can enter and be received as friends. It is a way of revealing oneself and God so that others may come to find him in their own way. The kind of hospitality that St. Paul spoke about to the Romans is based on the self-giving love that creates the space where others can feel at home and welcome, so that genuine love can take hold and spread. In a world full of hostility and alienation, more than ever people crave a place where they can live in a climate of affirmation and acceptance, where they can reveal themselves and experience the exchange of life and love that is the sign of the presence of the Risen Lord in the world. Christian spirituality relies on the free transfer of God's gifts to others in relationships, so that they may come to know God's healing, uplifting, guiding grace.

A blueprint for living out Christian values in marriage is found in the section of St. Matthew's Gospel called the Sermon on the Mount, in the part known as the Beatitudes. At first glance it may seem unusual that the first Gospel selection provided in the Catholic wedding ritual is Matthew's version of the Beatitudes (5:1-12), but on examination we can see that living out these values is a way to actualize a Christian witness in the world. Since the Beatitudes are such an essential guide for Christian life and love, we will devote particular attention to each individual saying as it relates to marital life and spirituality.

Matthew writes: "How blest are the poor in spirit: the reign of God is theirs" (5:3). To be poor in spirit cannot be measured in dollars and cents but is an inner disposition that calls persons to realize their own limitations and levels of need, and to put their trust in God. If a marriage is to flourish and grow in the midst of conflict and pain, it needs to be rooted in the love of the spouses for each other and in their mutual love of God. A couple can know great happiness if they possess the joy of knowing that they are loved by God and that his love has overflowed into their hearts. To be poor in spirit means, as Matthew points out elsewhere, to "seek first his kingship over you, his way of holiness"; then "all things will be given you besides" (6:33). In Matthew's mind, to seek first to live out the values of the Kingdom of God will pave the way for other blessings as well.

The second Beatitude is: "Blest too are the sorrowing; they shall be consoled" (5:4). Every human life and relationship knows pain and suffering. The word Matthew uses for those who mourn, the "sorrowing," is the strongest Greek word for lamenting the loss of the dearly departed. An old Arab proverb says, "All sunshine makes a desert." Paradoxically, out of sorrow the joy of God can come, and a person can comfort and show compassion to one who is suffering in such a way that new strength and beauty can enter the soul. This insight is reflected in the work of Dr. Elisabeth Kübler-Ross, as the title of one of her books, *Death: The Final Stage of Growth,* shows. Even the most wrenching of human experiences can have a redemptive value if not undergone alone. God sees, cares, and calls people to wholeness in the midst of human pain, and invites us to do the same.

To live in the presence of God's Spirit means to "bring glad tidings to the lowly, to heal the brokenhearted, . . . to comfort all who mourn" (Isaiah 61:1-2). Bringing the comfort of God's restoration to others is a key to Matthew's Gospel, which consistently echoes the vision of the Prophet Isaiah:

> Comfort, give comfort to my people,
> > says your God. . . .
> . . . prepare the way of the Lord.
> Make straight in the wasteland a highway
> > for our God.
> Every valley shall be filled in,
> > every mountain and hill shall be made low;
> The rugged land shall be made a plain,
> > the rough country, a broad valley.
> Then the glory of the Lord shall be revealed,
> > and all mankind shall see it together. (Isaiah 40:1-5)

Matthew wants us to see that even when our lives seem to be a jagged wasteland, the comforting presence of another can help to smooth things out and reveal God's healing presence and love. In essence, the second Beatitude means: Blessed are those who care intensely for the sorrows and sufferings and needs of others. To care and to respond are the cornerstones of Christian married life.

The third Beatitude reads: "Blest are the lowly; they shall inherit the land" (5:5). To speak of being lowly, or "meek," does not really capture the full flavor of what Matthew intends in this Beatitude. The word he uses, in its root form, means gentleness, a kind of happy balance between too much anger and too little. The word was originally applied to domesticated animals, in the sense that they are self-controlled and their actions are governed by another. Matthew, in applying the term to humans, used it to connote humility, acceptance of the need to learn, and of the continued exigency to strive after and be willing to offer and accept forgiveness. It means that persons should not shy away from being angry at appropriate times, though they should be willing to withhold or moderate anger at other times.

In any marriage there will invariably be outbursts of anger, and if couples are not free to express their anger one might wonder if they are truly able to communicate their love. But if their anger is of the brooding, festering variety it can only be a force for destruction in the relationship. Anger, channeled openly and gently in a constructive way, can be one of the most positive forces in a marriage relationship. Yet it can also be a source of terrible destruction if left unbridled or unchecked.

There is a great deal of wisdom in St. Paul's Letter to the Ephesians: "If you are angry, let it be without sin. The sun must not go down on your wrath; do not give the devil a chance to work on you. . . . Never let evil talk pass your lips; say only the good things men need to hear, things that will really help them. . . . Get rid of all bitterness, all passion and anger, harsh words, slander, and malice of every kind. In place of these, be kind to one another, compassionate, and mutually forgiving, just as God has forgiven you in Christ" (4:26,29,31-32). These words remind us that there is nothing sinful in anger *per se,* though it can lead into sin if it carries over and affects one's ability to be kind, compassionate, and mutually forgiving. Perhaps the best advice that can have long-range effect on the quality of a couple's marital happiness and spiritual growth is Paul's command not to let the sun set on one's anger. To be gentle, compassionate, and mutually forgiving is a challenging call, but it is the foundation of Christian married life on a day-in, day-out basis.

The fourth Beatitude is: "Blest are those who hunger and thirst for holiness; they shall have their fill" (5:6). A better translation for *holiness* in this verse is "righteousness" or "justice." This Beatitude stresses the "outer dimension" of Christian marriage, its orientation in service to the wider human family. Hunger for justice is a great concern in Matthew's Gospel. He uses the term for "righteousness" seven times.

The expression he uses for "hunger and thirst" calls up a vivid picture of a person who is starving and parched and who will die unless he or she gets food and drink. Matthew wants his readers to see that justice is an essential dimension of Christian life, in the tradition of the Prophet Micah:

> You have been told . . . what is good,
>> and what the Lord requires of you:
> Only to do the right and to love goodness,
>> and to walk humbly with your God. (6:8)

To act kindly, love justly, and walk humbly with God are truly the "be-attitudes" that Christian marriage calls for.

This hunger and thirst for righteousness refers not only to the outer dimension of marriage but to the relationship between the spouses as well. At times the couple will know brokenness, hurt, and distance in their relationship, but to strive for righteousness ensures genuine satisfaction of the couple's needs and the fulfillment of the promise of covenant love that binds the two as one. This Beatitude reminds us of the beautiful promise that Isaiah attributes to the Creator God:

> A bruised reed he shall not break,
>> and a smoldering wick he shall not quench,
> Until he establishes justice on the earth. (42:3-4)

Though at times a couple may feel bruised or smothered on account of the ways in which they interact with each other, if they hold out for seeking after God's righteousness as a priority, they are promised a full share of it in return.

The fifth Beatitude states: "Blest are they who show mercy; mercy shall be theirs" (5:7). Matthew's concern for showing mercy and forgiveness to others is a recurrent theme throughout his Gospel. It is a theme that pervades the entire Bible, and it means that we are to get right inside the skin of another person until we can see with his or her eyes, feel with his or her feelings, and think with his or her mind. Elsewhere in Matthew's Gospel, Jesus assures his hearers, "It is mercy I desire" (9:12). God's gift of Jesus to the world is a powerful witness to this value. When a spouse is able to get right inside the other and begins to think and feel the way the other does, frequently the other person is able to do the same for his or her spouse in turn. Mercy begets mercy. It is not a thing that can be earned, but a gift to be freely offered and longed for.

Paradoxically, a Christian cannot earn God's forgiveness but can lose it by stubbornly refusing to extend mercy to another. As Scripture scholar Father John Meier points out, to refuse a sister or brother the bonds of forgiveness that mark us as sons or daughters of God is "to rupture the family bond and break the lifeline of mercy binding us through Jesus to the Father. . . . The Church can continue to exist only if the men who are made brothers by this mercy can continue to exchange it—not with an external ritual gesture, but 'from the heart.'"

For St. Matthew, reconciliation is the foundational principle for life in the Kingdom of God, Jesus' first and last word on what it means to be a Christian in the world. In a marriage context, perhaps more than in any other human relationship, the depth of intimacy suggests that when healing and forgiveness are needed but are not offered, the intensity of the hurt is compounded. If a couple truly try to get inside each other's skin and see things from that perspective, the odds are good that they will be able to live in an understanding, compassionate, and forgiving way in spite of the wrongs and hurts they inflict upon each other.

The sixth Beatitude is: "Blest are the single-hearted, for they shall see God" (5:8). To be single-hearted, or pure of heart, means to center one's life on doing the work of God. In the ancient world, the heart was seen not only as the seat of one's emotions but also as the core of a person's being. Matthew wants his readers to see that if one places God and the values of his Kingdom uppermost in one's heart, one can know the presence of God. This is reflected in the Book of Psalms:

> Who can ascend the mountain of the Lord?
> or who may stand in his holy place?

He whose hands are sinless, whose heart is
    clean. . . .
He shall receive a blessing from the Lord. (24:3-5)

Matthew urges us to turn away from the drive for power, prestige, and possessions and to seek first the Kingdom of God: "Where your treasure is, there your heart is also" (6:21). Matthew promises that the pure of heart will one day see God face-to-face.

The seventh Beatitude reads: "Blest too are the peacemakers; they shall be called children of God" (5:9). The kind of peace spoken of here is not merely the absence of strife but encompasses everything that allows for our highest state of good. The peace of Christ is aimed toward giving us an experience of God's indwelling presence that reflects his unity of life. Jesus wills that all men and women share in his peace:

"Peace" is my farewell to you,
My peace is my gift to you;
I do not give it to you as the world gives
    peace.
Do not be distressed or fearful. (John 14:27)

To be a peacemaker is to work to produce right relationships among persons, enabling them to realize their full human potential as sons or daughters of God. Matthew sees this as a Godlike work and calls all Christians to strive for peace: "If your brother should commit some wrong against you, go and point out his fault, but keep it between the two of you. If he listens to you, you have won your brother over" (18:15). To be a peacemaker requires the investment of time and energy to bring about healing where there is brokenness. To do this is to do the work of God.

It is easy in any relationship to take steps that can lead not to peace but to conflict and intimate warfare. When a person feels threatened or hurt, the natural human tendency is to recoil and paint the other person into a corner as the "heavy," while trying to convice oneself of being in the right. The common response is to focus only on the extremes and to dwell on the other person's negative features, while refusing to show mercy or see things from the other person's perspective. As each side develops an overconfidence reflecting a distorted interpretation of reality, the prospects for conflict, rather than peacemaking, begin to flourish. This scenario can be avoided if the persons involved choose to foster and maintain right relationships among themselves, for in doing so they are doing the work of God.

The last of Matthew's eight Beatitudes is: "Blest are those persecuted for holiness' sake; the reign of God is theirs" (5:10). Matthew reminds us that to live a Christian life and Christian values can make a person the object of scorn and derision. At times it can serve as a source of conflict and tension at work, at home, in the neighborhood, or within one's social circle. In a like vein, the author of the First Letter of Peter writes: "In summary, then, all of you should be like-minded, sympathetic, loving toward one another, kindly disposed, and humble. Do not return evil for evil or insult for insult. Return a blessing instead. This you have been called to do, that you may receive a blessing as your inheritance. . . . Even if you should have to suffer for justice's sake, happy will you be. . . . Rejoice instead, in the measure that you share Christ's sufferings. When his glory is revealed, you will rejoice exultantly . . . for then God's Spirit in its glory has come to rest on you" (1 Peter 3:8-9,14; 4:13-14).

The Beatitudes contained in St. Matthew's Gospel in the Sermon on the Mount offer a plan for living out the everyday events of married life, and form a blueprint for setting out to achieve our destiny as sons and daughters made in the image and likeness of God.

Appendix

A PREMARITAL CHECKLIST

AT LEAST ONE YEAR PRIOR TO THE WEDDING

_____ Check out the frank perceptions of others concerning the prospects for your new marriage, especially those of children, other relatives, and friends.

_____ Take time to get to know your prospective spouse's children, if any, on an individual basis.

_____ Contact your parish priest to begin premarital preparation steps (such as filling out forms) and to reserve the date and time for the church ceremony.

_____ Investigate local marriage preparation programs for previously married persons. Good working models can be obtained by contacting:

1. Family Life Center
   Diocese of Toledo
   1933 Spielsbusch Ave.
   Toledo, OH 43624
2. Ministry to Separated and Divorced Catholics
   Family Development Centre
   Archdiocese of Ottawa
   256 King Edward Highway

Ottawa, Ontario
Canada K1N 7M1
3. The Beginning Experience (weekend renewal program, offered in most states)
   3100 W. 45th St.
   Sioux Falls, SD 57105

_____ Consider taking the PREPARE, P.M.I., or Myers-Briggs tests to measure compatibility with your prospective spouse. A useful treatment of such personality type indicator tests is found in Isabel Briggs Myers, *Gifts Differing* (Palo Alto, Cal.: Consulting Psychologists Press, 1979).

_____ Discuss with your prospective spouse the kind of wedding you want, how many guests to invite, and what the budgetary restrictions might be.

_____ Begin to work out a detailed budget for the wedding, reception, and honeymoon, and to discuss the financial aspects of the merged household.

_____ Talk to relatives, friends, and acquaintances who have previously remarried to determine what financial snags they have encountered and how they might best be avoided.

_____ Begin to discuss where the new, joint household will be, how it will be furnished, and how the household labor will be divided.

_____ Consider consulting a tax expert or matrimonial lawyer to explore tax and legal questions relating to your former and prospective marriages.

_____ Begin to plan the wedding attire for the bride and groom and members of the wedding party.

_____ Start to make arrangements for the reception hall, flowers, photography, transportation of the wedding party, and so forth.

THREE TO SIX MONTHS
PRIOR TO THE WEDDING

_____ Obtain copies of baptismal certificates issued within the past six months. First Communion and Confirmation notations should accompany these certificates.

_____ Obtain a letter from a priest in your home parish stating that you are free to marry and that permission has been granted for you to marry in the agreed-upon parish.

_____ Obtain any necessary dispensations (for mixed religion or from canonical form).

_____ Contact the parish music director to plan the music for the church ceremony.

_____ Set the time for the wedding rehearsal.

_____ Finalize the guest list.

_____ Order invitations, announcements, and thank-you notes from a printer.

_____ Meet with the celebrant to finalize plans for the ceremony.

_____ Shop for gifts for your spouse and for members of the wedding party.

_____ Shop for wedding rings.

_____ Begin to plan music for the reception.

ONE MONTH BEFORE THE WEDDING

_____ Mail out the invitations.

_____ Be fitted for wedding gowns and suits.

_____ Arrange for a rehearsal dinner, if desired.

_____ Make out new wills.

_____ Buy new luggage and clothing for the honeymoon, if needed.

_____ Obtain marriage license from Town Hall and take blood tests, if required.

_____ Finalize moving plans.

_____ Make transportation arrangements for the honeymoon.

_____ Begin to finalize the total number of reception guests.

_____ Inform the appropriate sources of upcoming changes in name and/or address for driver's licenses, charge cards, Social Security cards, passports, insurance policies, magazine subscriptions, and the like.

_____ Make an appointment with your barber or hairdresser.

ONE WEEK BEFORE THE WEDDING

_____ Notify the reception hall of the final number of guests.

_____ Confirm the rehearsal time with the celebrant. Be prepared to bring fees and the license to the rehearsal.

_____ Have the photographer check with the celebrant concerning any restrictions.

_____ Start packing for the honeymoon.

_____ Check on floral arrangements.

_____ Arrange for lectors, if any, to practice readings before the ceremony.

_____ Finalize liturgical details with the celebrant.

BIBLIOGRAPHY

Chapter 1 THE END OF A MARRIAGE: A CRISIS OF LOSS

Gardner, Richard. *The Parents' Book About Divorce*. New York: Bantam Books, 1979.

Krantzler, Mel. *Creative Divorce*. New York: Signet, 1975.

Kübler-Ross, Elisabeth. *On Death and Dying*. New York: Macmillan, 1969.

Weiss, Robert. *Marital Separation*. New York: Basic Books, 1975.

Chapter 2 FEELINGS TRIGGERED BY A BROKEN MARRIAGE

Gardner, Richard. *The Parents' Book About Divorce*. New York: Bantam Books, 1979.

Kennedy, Eugene. *On Becoming a Counselor*. New York: Continuum, 1980.

Krantzler, Mel. *Creative Divorce*. New York: Signet, 1975.

Kübler-Ross, Elisabeth. *Questions and Answers on Death and Dying*. New York: Macmillan, 1974.

Marshall, George. *Facing Death and Grief*. Buffalo: Prometheus Books, 1981.

Weiss, Robert. *Marital Separation*. New York: Basic Books, 1975.

Chapter 3 EMOTIONAL ADJUSTMENT: COPING WITH ANXIETY, DEPRESSION, ANGER, GUILT, AND LONELINESS

Gardner, Richard. *The Parents' Book About Divorce*. New York: Bantam Books, 1979.

Kennedy, Eugene. *Crisis Counseling*. New York: Continuum, 1981.

Krantzler, Mel. *Creative Divorce*. New York: Signet, 1975.

Kübler-Ross, Elisabeth. *Living with Death and Dying*. New York: Macmillan, 1981.

Young, James. *Growing Through Divorce*. New York: Paulist Press, 1979.

Chapter 4 THE NATURE OF CHRISTIAN MARRIAGE

Bassett, William, ed. *The Bond of Marriage*. Notre Dame, Ind.: University of Notre Dame Press, 1968.

Haughton, Rosemary. *The Theology of Marriage*. Butler, Wis.: Clergy Book Service, 1971.

Kasper, Walter. *Theology of Christian Marriage*. New York: Seabury Press, 1980.

Whitehead, Evelyn and James. *Marrying Well: Possibilities in Christian Marriage Today*. New York: Doubleday, 1981.

Chapter 5 BIBLICAL APPROACHES TO DIVORCE AND REMARRIAGE

Crossan, Dominic. "Divorce and Remarriage in the New Testament," in William Bassett, ed., *The Bond of Marriage*. Notre Dame, Ind.: University of Notre Dame Press, 1968.

Haughton, Rosemary. *The Theology of Marriage*. Butler, Wis.: Clergy Book Service, 1971.

MacRae, George. "New Testament Perspectives on Marriage and Divorce," in James Young, ed., *Ministering to the Divorced Catholic*. New York: Paulist Press, 1979.

Chapter 6 IS MARRIAGE FOREVER?

Green, Thomas J. "Canonical-Pastoral Reflections on Divorce and Remarriage," in James Young, ed., *Ministering to the Divorced Catholic*. New York: Paulist Press, 1979.

Kasper, Walter. *Theology of Christian Marriage*. New York: Seabury Press, 1979.

Kelleher, Stephen. "Can Marriage Die?" *Origins,* June 20, 1974, pp. 53-56.

McCormick, Richard. "Indissolubility and the Right to the Eucharist," in James Young, ed., *Ministering to the Divorced Catholic*. New York: Paulist Press, 1979.

Wrenn, Lawrence, ed. *Divorce and Remarriage in the Catholic Church*. New York: Newman Press, 1973.

Chapter 7 THE ORTHODOX "PRINCIPLE OF ECONOMY"

Curran, Charles. "Divorce from the Perspective of Moral Theology." *Origins,* November 14, 1974, pp. 329-335.

Maloney, George A., S.J. "Oeconomia: A Corrective to Law," *Catholic Lawyer* 17, 1971, pp. 90-109.

Orsy, Ladislas, S.J. "In Search of the Meaning of *Oikonomia*: Report on a Convention," *Theological Studies* 43, June, 1982, pp. 312-319.

Patsavos, Lewis. "The Orthodox Position on Divorce," in James Young, ed., *Ministering to the Divorced Catholic*. New York: Paulist Press, 1979.

Schmemann, Alexander. "The Indissolubility of Marriage: The Theological Tradition of the East," in William Bassett, ed., *The Bond of Marriage*. Notre Dame, Ind.: University of Notre Dame Press, 1968.

Stephanopoulos, Robert. "Orthodox View." *Origins,* June 20, 1974, pp. 56-57.

Chapter 8 THE ANNULMENT PROCESS

Finnegan, John T. "Marriage," in "The Pastoral Guide to Canon Law." *Chicago Studies,* Fall, 1976, pp. 281-304.

Green, Thomas J. "Canonical-Pastoral Reflections on Divorce and Remarriage," in James Young, ed., *Ministering to the Divorced Catholic.* New York: Paulist Press, 1979.

Green, Thomas J. "Psychological Grounds for Church Annulments: Changing Canonical Practice." *Social Thought,* Spring, 1978, pp. 47-59.

Hudson, Edward. *Handbook for Marriage Nullity Cases.* Ottawa: St. Paul's University, 1976.

Tierney, Terence. *Annulment: Do You Have a Case?* New York: Alba House, 1978.

Wrenn, Lawrence. *Annulments.* Toledo: Canon Law Society of America, 1978 revision.

Chapter 9 THE INTERNAL FORUM SOLUTION

Catoir, John D. "When the Courts Don't Work," *America* 25, 1971, pp. 254-257.

Curran, Charles. "Divorce From the Perspective of Moral Theology." *Origins,* November 14, 1974, pp. 329-335.

Finnegan, John T. "Marriage," in "The Pastoral Guide to Canon Law." *Chicago Studies,* Fall, 1976, pp. 281-304.

Finnegan, John T. "Spiritual Direction for the Catholic Divorced and Remarried," *Proceedings of the Canon Law Society of America,* 1973, pp. 70-83. Also in Young, *Ministering to the Divorced Catholic,* pp. 122-137.

Gantner, Bishop Bernard. "Letter from Bishop Gantner." *Divorce,* Spring, 1979, pp. 3-6.

Green, Thomas J. "Ministering to Marital Failure," *Chicago Studies* 18, Fall, 1979, pp. 327-344.

Lehmann, Karl. "Indissolubility of Marriage, and Pastoral Care of the Divorced Who Remarry," in James Young, ed., *Ministering to the Divorced Catholic.* New York: Paulist Press, 1979.

Chapter 10 EXCOMMUNICATION AND ACCESS TO THE EUCHARIST

Finnegan, John. "Marriage/Pastoral Care." *Origins,* August 25, 1975, pp. 155-158.

Green, Thomas J. "Ministering to Marital Failure." *Chicago Studies,* Fall, 1979, pp. 327-344.

McCormick, Richard. "Indissolubility and the Right to the Eucharist," in James Young, ed., *Ministering to the Divorced Catholic.* New York: Paulist Press, 1979.

O'Donnell, Bishop Cletus. "Bishops Vote to Repeal Excommunication," in James Young, ed., *Ministering to the Divorced Catholic.* New York: Paulist Press, 1979.

Provost, James H. "Intolerable Marriage Situations Revisited," *The Jurist* 40:1, 1980, pp. 141-224.

Ripple, Paula. *The Pain and the Possibility: Divorce and Separation Among Catholics.* Notre Dame, Ind.: Ave Maria Press, 1978.

Young, James. *When You're Divorced and Catholic.* St. Meinrad, Ind.: Abbey Press, 1981.

Chapter 11 PROSPECTS FOR A SUCCESSFUL MARRIAGE TODAY

Glick, Paul. "A Demographer Looks at American Families," in James Young, ed., *Ministering to the Divorced Catholic.* New York: Paulist Press, 1979.

Ripple, Paula. *The Pain and the Possibility: Divorce and Separation Among Catholics.* Notre Dame, Ind.: Ave Maria Press, 1978.

Weiss, Robert. *Marital Separation.* New York: Basic Books, 1975.

Young, James. *Growing Through Divorce.* New York: Paulist Press, 1979.

Chapter 12 DATING AGAIN

Gardner, Richard. *The Parents' Book About Divorce*. New York: Bantam Books, 1979.

Krantzler, Mel. *Learning to Love Again*. New York: Avon Books, 1979.

Weiss, Robert. *Marital Separation*. New York: Basic Books, 1975.

Chapter 13 DEALING WITH SEXUALITY

Doherty, Dennis, ed. *Dimensions of Human Sexuality*. New York: Doubleday, 1979.

Greeley, Andrew. *Sexual Intimacy*. New York: Seabury Press, 1973.

Haughton, Rosemary. *The Holiness of Sex*. St. Meinrad, Ind.: Abbey Press, 1969.

Keane, Philip S., S.S. *Sexual Morality: A Catholic Perspective*. New York: Paulist Press, 1977.

Kennedy, Eugene. *Sexual Counseling*. New York: Continuum, 1980.

Taylor, Michael, ed. *Sex: Thoughts for Contemporary Christians*. New York: Doubleday Image, 1973.

Chapter 14 MAKING A PERMANENT COMMITMENT: ASSESSING NEEDS AND MATCHING PERSONALITIES

Haessly, Jacqueline and DiDomizio, Daniel. "Expectations in Marriage," in Celine Allen and Charles Keating, eds., *Preparing for Marriage*. New York: Paulist Press, 1980.

Krantzler, Mel. *Creative Divorce*. New York: Signet Books, 1979.

Krantzler, Mel. *Learning to Love Again*. New York: Avon Books, 1979.

Mace, David. *Getting Ready for Marriage*. Nashville: Abingdon Press, 1972.

Weiss, Robert. *Marital Separation*. New York: Basic Books, 1975.

Chapter 15 INTERFAITH MARRIAGES

Aridas, Christopher. *Your Catholic Wedding*. New York: Doubleday Image, 1982.

Finnegan, John T. "Marriage," in "The Pastoral Guide to Canon Law." *Chicago Studies,* Fall, 1976, pp. 292-293.

Haskin, Jay C. "The Catholic Pastor and the Pastoral Care of Interchurch Couples and Their Families," *The Priest* 38, July-August, 1982, pp. 12-14.

"Mixed Marriage." *The National Bulletin on Liturgy,* May/June, 1977, pp. 161-165.

Rebeck, Theresa. "Two Faiths in One Family: How the Ecumenical Marriage Survives." *St. Anthony Messenger,* January, 1981, pp. 16-21.

Schiappa, Barbara. *Mixing: Catholic-Protestant Marriages in the 1980's/A Guidebook for Couples and Families*. New York: Paulist Press, 1982.

Thomas, John. *Beginning Your Marriage: Interfaith Edition*. Chicago: Buckley Publications, 1980.

Chapter 16 MARRYING OUTSIDE THE CHURCH

"Christological Theses on the Sacrament of Marriage." *Origins,* September 14, 1978, pp. 202-204.

Kasper, Walter. *Theology of Christian Marriage*. New York: Seabury Press, 1980.

"Propositions on the Doctrine of Christian Marriage." *Origins,* July 28, 1978, pp. 238-240.

Chapter 17 PLANNING THE CEREMONY

Aridas, Christopher. *Your Catholic Wedding*. New York: Doubleday Image, 1982.

Champlin, Joseph. *Together for Life*. Notre Dame, Ind.: Ave Maria Press, 1975 revision.

Harrington, Jeremy. *Your Wedding: Planning Your Own Ceremony*. Cincinnati: St. Anthony Messenger Press, 1974.

Wall, Wendy. *The Creative Wedding Handbook*. New York: Paulist Press, 1972.

Chapter 18 RELATING TO THE NEW EXTENDED FAMILY

Gardner, Richard. *The Boys' and Girls' Book About Divorce*. New York: Bantam Books, 1978.

Gardner, Richard. *The Boys' and Girls' Book About Step-Families*. New York: Bantam Books, 1982.

Gardner, Richard. *The Parents' Book About Divorce*. New York: Bantam Books, 1979.

Krantzler, Mel. *Learning to Love Again*. New York: Avon Books, 1979.

Stewart, Marjabelle Young. *Getting Married Again*. New York: Avon Books, 1981.

Weiss, Robert. *Marital Separation*. New York: Basic Books, 1975.

Chapter 19 ESTABLISHING A NEW HOUSEHOLD

Krantzler, Mel. *Learning to Love Again*. New York: Avon Books, 1979.

Stewart, Marjabelle Young. *Getting Married Again*. New York: Avon Books, 1981.

Weiss, Robert. *Marital Separation*. New York: Basic Books, 1975.

Chapter 20 FINANCIAL MATTERS

Hodes, Marion. "Finances," in Celine Allen and Charles Keating, eds., *Preparing for Marriage*. New York: Paulist Press, 1980.

Krantzler, Mel. *Learning to Love Again*. New York: Avon Books, 1979.

Rogers, Mary. *Women, Divorce, and Money*. New York: McGraw-Hill, 1981.

Thomas, John. *Beginning Your Marriage*. Chicago: Buckley Publications, 1980.

Weiss, Robert. *Marital Separation*. New York: Basic Books, 1975.

Chapter 21 FAMILY PLANNING

Butler, B.C. "Authority and the Christian Conscience," *The Clergy Review* 60, January, 1975, pp. 3-17.

Callahan, Daniel, ed. *The Catholic Case for Contraception*. New York: Macmillan, 1969.

Curran, Charles E. *Themes in Fundamental Moral Theology*. Notre Dame, Ind.: University of Notre Dame Press, 1973.

Gula, Richard M., S.S. *What Are They Saying About Moral Norms?* New York: Paulist Press, 1981.

Häring, Bernard. *Free and Faithful in Christ: Volume II*. New York: Seabury Press, 1979.

Keane, Philip S., S.S. *Sexual Morality: A Catholic Perspective*. New York: Paulist Press, 1977.

Kipley, John and Sheila. *The Art of Natural Family Planning*. Cincinnati: CCL Books, 1979.

McBrien, Richard P. *Catholicism*. Minneapolis: Winston Press, 1980.

Nelson, C. Ellis, ed. *Conscience: Theological and Psychological Perspectives*. New York: Newman Press, 1973.

Noonan, John. *The Church and Contraception: The Issues at Stake*. New York: Paulist Press, 1967.

O'Connell, Timothy E. *Principles for a Catholic Morality.* New York: Seabury Press, 1978.

Quinn, Archbishop John. "Contraception: A Proposal for the Synod." *Catholic Mind,* February, 1981, pp. 25-28.

Chapter 22 UNDERSTANDING THE STAGES OF MARRIAGE

Joyce, Gerald, and Zullo, James. "Ministry to Marital Growth: A Developmental Perspective." *Chicago Studies,* Fall, 1979, pp. 263-277.

Krantzler, Mel. *Creative Marriage.* New York: McGraw-Hill, 1981.

Levinson, Daniel, et al. *The Seasons of a Man's Life.* New York: Random House, 1978.

Sheehy, Gail. *Passages: Predictable Crises of Adult Life.* New York: Dutton, 1976.

Whitehead, Evelyn and James. *Christian Life Patterns: The Psychological Challenges and Religious Invitations of Adult Life.* New York: Doubleday Image, 1982.

Chapter 23 ONGOING MARRIAGE ENRICHMENT AND CONFLICT RESOLUTION

Clinebell, Howard and Charlotte. *The Intimate Marriage.* New York: Harper & Row, 1970.

Greeley, Andrew. *Sexual Intimacy.* New York: Seabury Press, 1973.

Hunt, Morton. "Strengthening Marriage the 'No-Fault' Way." *Families,* May, 1982, pp. 48-51.

Krantzler, Mel. *Creative Marriage.* New York: McGraw-Hill, 1981.

Mace, David and Vera. *How to Have a Happy Marriage: A Step-by-Step Guide to an Enriched Relationship.* Nashville: Abingdon, 1977.

Masters, William, and Johnson, Virginia. *The Pleasure Bond: A New Look at Sexuality and Commitment*. Boston: Little, Brown and Company, 1974.

Miller, Maureen. "Creative Conflict," in Celine Allen and Charles Keating, eds., *Preparing for Marriage*. New York: Paulist Press, 1980.

St. Aelred of Rievaulx. *On Spiritual Friendship*. Kalamazoo, Mich.: Cistercian Publications, 1976.

Satir, Virginia. *Conjoint Family Therapy*. Palo Alto, Cal.: Science and Behavior Books, 1972.

Satir, Virginia. *Peoplemaking*. Palo Alto, Cal.: Science and Behavior Books, 1972.

Chapter 24 TOWARD A MARITAL SPIRITUALITY

Crosby, Michael. *Spirituality of the Beatitudes: Matthew's Challenge for First World Christians*. Maryknoll, N.Y.: Orbis Books, 1980.

Leckey, Dolores R. *The Ordinary Way: A Family Spirituality*. New York: Crossroad Publishing Company, 1981.

Lewis, C.S. *The Four Loves*. New York: Harcourt Brace Jovanovich, 1960.

Nouwen, Henri. *Reaching Out: Three Movements of the Solitary Life*. New York: Doubleday, 1975.

Whitehead, Evelyn and James. *Marrying Well: Possibilities in Christian Marriage Today*. New York: Doubleday, 1981.